METEORITES

Caroline Smith, Sara Russell
and Gretchen Benedix

Published by the Natural History Museum, London

This book is dedicated to the memory of Dr Robert Hutchison (1938-2007), former Head of Meteorites at the Natural History Museum. Robert was a colleague, friend and mentor who had an encyclopaedic knowledge of meteorites and always found time to share it.

First published by the Natural History Museum, Cromwell Road, London SW7 5BD
© Natural History Museum, London, 2009

ISBN 978 0 565 09239 9

A catalogue record for this book is available from the British Library.

Copy-edited by Karin Fancett
Designed by Mercer Design, London
Reproduction by Saxon Digital Services
Printing by C&C Offset Printing Co. Ltd.

Front cover image: The Esquel pallasite, composed of gem-quality olivine crystals embedded in metal. Pallasites are perhaps the most beautiful of all meteorites. © NHMPL.
Title page: Leonid meteorite shower. © Dr Fred Espenak/Science Photo Library.
Back cover image; Shooting star. © NHMPL.

Find out more about Publishing at the Natural History Museum
www.nhm.ac.uk/publishing

CONTENTS

WHAT ARE
METEORITES?

METEORITES ARE NATURAL OBJECTS COMPOSED of stone, metal or a mixture of metal and stone that survive their fall from space to land on the Earth. Most meteorites originate from asteroids, a few come from the planet Mars or the moon, and some may even come from comets. Meteorites from asteroids are the oldest objects available for study, dating back to the very first stages of solar system formation, about 4,570 million years ago. The study of meteorites provides a window back in time, so we can learn about the processes that formed and shaped the solar system, and the planets, moons, asteroids and comets it contains, including our own Earth.

Meteorites are divided into three main types on the basis of their composition. Stone meteorites are composed mainly of silicate minerals similar to those found in rocks on Earth. Iron meteorites are composed of iron metal alloyed with nickel. Stony-iron meteorites, as their name suggests, are composed of a mixture of iron–nickel metal and silicate minerals. These different meteorite types are further described in chapter 4.

OPPOSITE Weighing in at 60 t plus, the Hoba meteorite is the largest known on Earth.

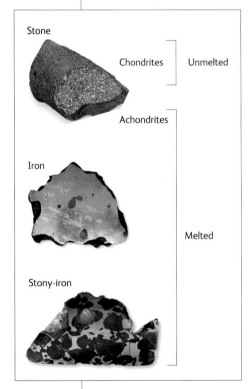

ABOVE The three main types of meteorite: stone, iron and stony-iron. Irons and stony-irons are the product of melting, as are stony achondrites. Chondrites have not melted since they first aggregated.

METEORS, METEOROIDS, FIREBALLS AND METEORITES

About 40,000–60,000 t of extraterrestrial material falls on the Earth every year. Before entering Earth's atmosphere these fragments are known as meteoroids, and individual pieces can range in size from tiny, microscopic grains of dust to large bodies, many metres in diameter. The vast majority of the material that lands on Earth is in the form of tiny dust grains, usually less than 1 mm (1/25 in) in size, known as cosmic dust, micrometeorites or interplanetary dust particles (IDPs). Because these objects are so small, they radiate away the frictional heating produced as they pass through the atmosphere faster than they melt, and thus survive intact to land on Earth.

ABOVE AND RIGHT An interplanetary dust particle collected in the atmosphere (above, field of view is about 25 μm) and a cosmic spherule collected from the Antarctic ice (right, field of view is about 60 μm). Tens of thousands of tons of material like this falls to Earth each year.

You may have been lucky enough to have seen a meteor or 'shooting star'. These streaks of light are produced by larger objects, perhaps the size of a small pebble. The effects of frictional heating as such objects pass through Earth's atmosphere are great enough to melt and vaporize the material, producing a very rapid, bright streak in the night sky. At some times during the year many meteors can be observed over a period of a few days. These 'meteor showers' are related to the orbits of known comets and occur at well-defined times during the year (see chapter 5). Meteors do not result in meteorites. It is extremely rare for material from a meteor to be recovered on Earth.

RIGHT Scientists collecting an ice core in Antarctica in order to extract micrometeorites.

LEFT The Peekskill meteorite was witnessed by many people as it partially burned up in the atmosphere.

BELOW The fusion crust of a meteorite is a thin coating that may be glassy or matt in appearance.

If still larger fragments (many centimetres or even metres in size) enter Earth's atmosphere they can produce spectacular light and sound effects as they fall. As they pass through the Earth's atmosphere these are called fireballs. Meteorites may land on Earth as a result of a large meteoroid entering the Earth's atmosphere. A meteoroid travels in space at its cosmic velocity, about 30 km/s (67,500 mph). When it reaches the Earth's atmosphere it is slowed down by friction and these frictional forces also act on its outermost surface, heating it to melting temperature.

Only the outermost surface of the meteoroid melts and the resulting droplets of molten material are carried away as the meteoroid speeds through the atmosphere. (This is unlike meteors, where the entire object is vaporized and destroyed.) The rapid speed of the meteoroid as it enters the atmosphere also generates shock waves (sonic booms), which are often heard as explosions. As the meteoroid is further slowed down by the atmosphere it begins to cool rapidly and its molten surface forms a glassy coating called the fusion crust. Finally, it falls to the ground under the influence of gravity and is now termed a meteorite.

METEOROIDS, METEORS AND METEORITES

A meteoroid is a small body, typically less than hundreds of kilogrammes in mass, travelling through space that may, or may not land on Earth as a meteorite.

A meteor or 'shooting star' is a vivid streak of light produced when a small meteoroid, perhaps up to a few centimetres in size, enters the Earth's atmosphere and completely vaporizes through frictional heating.

Meteorites are natural objects made of rock, metal or a mixture of rock and metal that survive their fall from space to land on the Earth.

Sometimes one side of the meteorite may be curved or even conical in shape. This is the 'leading edge' of the meteorite, the side that pointed in the direction the meteoroid travelled during its passage through the atmosphere. If the meteorite has tumbled during its flight it will have a more irregular shape, although it should still retain rounded edges. Note that only the outermost surface of the meteoroid melts, while the interior remains cold and unchanged. Meteorites are almost always cold when they land. The very few reports of meteorites that have been recovered almost immediately after landing state that they are cold or slightly warm at most.

Meteorites fall more or less randomly over the Earth's surface and a number of studies have been carried out to estimate how many meteorites land on Earth every year. Some studies use cameras to image the night sky and record the number of observed fireballs, while other studies use the number of meteorites found in desert regions. Estimates indicate approximately 5,000 to 17,000 meteorites larger than 100 g (3 ½ oz) – about the size of a golf ball – fall on Earth every year. However, it is important to remember that 70% of the Earth's surface is covered by water and any meteorites landing in the oceans are unlikely ever to be recovered. Similarly, many parts of the world remain uninhabited or only have sparsely distributed populations, so any meteorites landing in these areas are unlikely to be seen by anyone.

BELOW The conical shape points in the direction of travel during atmospheric flight. The ridges that flow away from the centre were produced by ablation during entry.

LEFT A 36.7 g (2 oz) fragment of the Chergach meteorite, which fell in Mali in July 2007. Local people reported seeing a smoke cloud and hearing detonations, and seeing stars fall from the sky.

Every year only a handful of meteorites are witnessed to fall and are then recovered – these are known as 'fall' meteorites. In 2007, for example, there were seven authenticated 'fall' meteorites reported.

In some places, however, meteorites can be preserved or concentrated by natural processes. Most meteorites contain some proportion of metal, and the arid conditions found in the hot and cold deserts help to preserve them by slowing down the weathering and rusting that destroys the meteorites. Hot and cold deserts have provided extremely fertile meteorite hunting grounds, with tens of thousands of meteorites recovered so far. Meteorites that are found after they fell, either by chance or during dedicated collecting trips, are termed 'find' meteorites. Meteorite falls and finds are discussed further in chapter 2.

THE STUDY OF METEORITES – FIREBALLS AND THUNDERSTONES

Meteors, fireballs and meteorite falls have been observed and recorded since ancient times. Chinese astronomers recorded meteor showers around 700 BC, and objects including daggers and jewellery made from meteoritic iron have been recovered from Egyptian pyramids, including the famous tomb of Tutankhamen. In 1928, archaeologists excavating a prehistoric Native American settlement near the town of Winona in northern Arizona excavated a 24-kg (53-lb) meteorite that had been carefully buried in a purpose-built crypt, or 'cist'. The archaeological setting suggests that the builders of the settlement treated the meteorite as an important object. However, the Sinagua tribe were only in the area for around 200 years from the eleventh century, and therefore the meteorite is unlikely to have been a witnessed fall.

ABOVE The yellow-green desert glass scarab in the middle of one of Tutankhamen's necklaces is made of glass, which was traced to a remote region of the Sahara Desert. It has been suggested that an aerial explosion of an incoming object over the desert created enough heat to turn the sand to glass.

The oldest meteorite seen to fall, and which is still preserved, is the Nogata meteorite that fell in the garden of the Suga Jinja Shinto shrine in Japan, over 1,100 years ago. Realizing the importance of the object, the shrine priests preserved it in a box as a special treasure. Although no written records exist, the story of the fall was passed down through the generations. In 1922, the head priest contacted a local geologist to ask his opinion on the stone and the geologist declared that it was indeed a meteorite. Then, in 1979, analyzes on a small piece of the stone confirmed this.

The first meteorite fall for which written records exist is the Ensisheim meteorite, which fell on the village of Ensisheim (now in the Alsace region of France) in 1492. A large fireball was observed and, after a large explosion, which caused much fright and excitement amongst the local people, a 127-kg (280-lb) stone fell on Ensisheim. This event was deemed so unusual and important it was recorded at the time in an engraving and was reported to the Emperor Maximillian, who ordered that the stone be preserved in the village church. The stone can still be seen in Ensisheim although it now resides in the town hall.

Between the fall of the Ensisheim meteorite and the late 1700s a number of meteorites were seen to fall and were recovered, although they were considered to be little worthy of scientific study. The modern study and science of meteorites (termed meteoritics) really began in 1768 when a stone that was claimed 'fell from the sky' over the town of Lucé, France, was presented to the Abbé Bachelay. The Abbé collected a number of eyewitness reports of the stone's fall and recovery and also wrote a detailed report, which he then passed on to the French Academy of

RIGHT The Ensisheim meteorite, which fell in 1492. Its fall was recorded in drawings and engravings and the stone was preserved. The stone can now be seen in the town hall in Ensisheim, France.

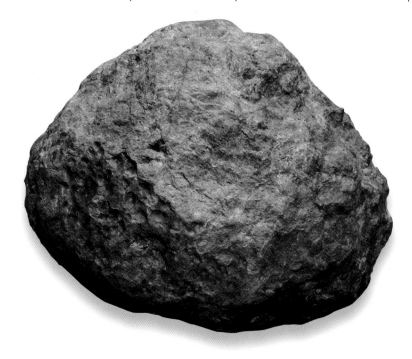

Sciences. The Academy set up a commission of enquiry, which included the famous French scientist Antoine Lavoisier, to study the stone and the Abbé's report.

The commission undertook the first chemical analyzes of a meteorite. They recognized the presence of iron sulphide and concluded that the stone was simply a terrestrial pyrite (pyrite, chemical formula FeS_2, is also known as 'fool's gold'). To account for the eyewitness reports of its fall and the presence of a black fusion crust, the scientists stated that the stone must have been struck by lightning, and consequently, meteorites were commonly referred to as 'thunderstones'. A report by such an eminent group of scientists received wide acceptance among the intellectual elite of Europe. Scientists were unwilling to believe in a phenomenon for which no witnesses of suitably high social rank could be found, and for which no reasonable scientific theories could be provided. Until the end of the eighteenth century meteorites remained to be seen by the scientific community as 'nothing out of the ordinary', and some people even advocated their destruction!

A number of well-witnessed meteorite falls occurred between 1789 and 1803, and these generated many publications of books, articles and pamphlets to explain their nature and origin. In 1794, the German physicist Ernst Chladni published a short book on meteorites. In this book, he described the characteristics of a number of unusual iron masses and descriptions of meteors, fireballs and witnessed falls of stones and irons, and concluded that that they were extraterrestrial in origin.

ABOVE The German scientist, Ernst Chladni (1756-1827) was the first to propose that meteorites are extraterrestrial in origin and is one of the founders of the modern scientific study of meteorites.

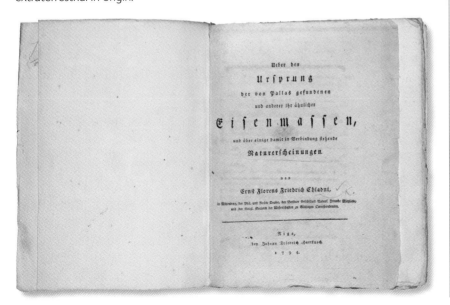

LEFT The title page of Ernst Chladni's book *On the Origin of the Pallas Iron and Others Similar to it, and on Some Associated Natural Phenomena*, which was published in 1794.

The year 1794 also marked the fall of the Siena meteorite in Italy. This event generated much interest in the English expatriate community, the majority of whom came from the upper echelons of English society, who were living in Italy or visiting it as part of the 'Grand Tour'. Travellers returning to England brought with them specimens of the meteorite (indeed, a thriving market grew up selling bogus 'fallen stones' to tourists), and fascinating stories regarding the shower of stones over the town.

Just a year later, in 1795, a large stone meteorite fell on farmland at Wold Cottage in Yorkshire, England. The event was witnessed by several people, loud explosions were heard and a young ploughman, John Shipley, witnessed the stone fall through the clouds and on to the ground very close to him. The local landowner, Captain Edward Topham, obtained sworn eyewitness testimonies from three people who had witnessed the fall and from others who had heard the explosions. Early in 1796 a detailed account, submitted by Topham, was published in the local newspaper and he later took the stone to London, where it was exhibited to the public. One of the visitors was the famous British naturalist and President of the Royal Society Sir Joseph Banks, and he obtained a sample of the stone. Banks decided that serious scientific investigation of meteorites should be carried out and so he passed his Wold Cottage fragment, along with samples of other meteorites, to the chemist Edward Howard. Howard discovered that all the samples contained nickel dissolved in iron, a characteristic that was not observed in any terrestrial rocks. Like Chladni, he concluded that an extraterrestrial origin was plausible.

The reports of Edward Howard's analyzes caused many European chemists and mineralogists to re-investigate samples reported to have fallen from the sky. Any remaining doubts, held by the scientific elite of Europe, that the fall of meteorites was a real phenomenon were quashed when a spectacular meteorite shower of over

3,000 stones fell over L'Aigle, France, in 1803. However, where meteorites formed was still a matter of debate, with two main theories competing in the scientific discussions of the early to mid-nineteenth century. Some scientists believed that the stones formed in the upper parts of the Earth's atmosphere, while others believed that they were formed as the result of volcanic explosions on the moon. It is important to stress that at this time the Earth-moon system was considered to be 'closed' (i.e. nothing could be added or lost), and that all atmospheric and weather phenomena (e.g. clouds, rain, hail, meteors, fireballs etc.) were part of this system. Chladni's theory that meteorites were truly extraterrestrial, originating outside the Earth-moon system in cosmic space, was still little believed.

Continued investigation of newly fallen meteorites in the early to mid-nineteenth century revealed that not all meteorites had the same chemistries or textures, or contained the same minerals, which suggested that they could not all originate from one place (i.e. the moon). During the same period, advances in telescope design and manufacture allowed astronomers to study the moon in ever increasing detail, with the result that few astronomers believed that lunar volcanoes were still active. Added to this was the finding that meteorites entered the Earth's atmosphere at cosmic velocities and, therefore, too high a velocity to be of lunar origin. Finally, since their initial discovery in 1801, an increasing number of asteroids were being observed, which were then thought to be the remains of a fragmented planet. It did not seem unreasonable to suggest that some of these fragments could land on Earth as meteorites, and the German scientist Alexander von Humboldt even called meteorites 'the smallest of all asteroids' in 1849.

With meteorites firmly being established as coming from space, their precise origin was still a matter of debate from the mid-1800s until as recently as the 1950s (interestingly the Martian origin of the 'SNC' group of meteorites was only firmly settled in the 1980s, see p.79). An interstellar origin (i.e. coming from outside our solar system) for some meteorites was suggested. However, this theory was dismissed with the precise measurement of velocities and orbits for meteorite parent bodies, which showed that they must have originated within the solar system.

Meteorites, rightly, are now recognized as being rare and precious samples of bodies within our solar system. They record a wealth of information about the birth and growth of the solar system, the formation and history of planets, and the role of impacts in shaping and modifying planets, asteroids and moons, and even record evidence of astrophysical processes that occurred long before our solar system was born.

WHERE ARE METEORITES FOUND?

EVERY YEAR THOUSANDS OF METEORITES land on Earth. Meteorites have been recovered from every continent of the Earth. In some places, where the environment and geography are favourable to meteorites being preserved and concentrated, many thousands of meteorites have been found. Meteorites that are witnessed to fall (often after people have observed spectacular fireballs and heard loud explosions) and are subsequently recovered, are known as meteorite 'falls'. As of January 2009, there have been 1,074 authenticated meteorite falls.

Meteorites which are found either accidentally or during a meteorite collecting trip are known as 'finds'. By January 2009, there were roughly 36,000 recorded find meteorites. Meteorites are usually named after the nearest town or geographical location where they fell or were found. In hot and cold desert regions, where many thousands of meteorites can be found in a relatively small area, they are given a name relating to the geographic region and a number (e.g. Allan Hills 84001, Dhofar 342).

OPPOSITE The arid climate and desert landscape of the Nullarbor Desert, Western Australia make it an ideal location to hunt for meteorites.

LEFT Part of the Barwell meteorite, which fell on Christmas Eve 1965, smashed through a window as it landed.

METEORITE FALLS

The rate of meteorite falls can be calculated using observations of fireballs and meteors. Data show that meteorites fall almost evenly around the globe, although meteorites are slightly less likely to fall at the poles than at the equator, because the parent meteoroids are likely to be travelling in the same plane as the planets. Meteorites can fall at any time of the day, but observations suggest that more meteorites fall in the afternoon and evening. This may be because at this point in its rotation, the Earth is facing in the same direction as it is travelling around the sun, therefore, meteorites are much more likely to fall (much in the same way as flies are more likely to stick to the front window of a car as it is travelling forwards).

Before the mid-twentieth century, the statistics of meteorite falls relied solely on eyewitness reports. Although these reports are often extremely detailed and provided by reliable witnesses, it must be remembered that a number of human and social factors can skew the data. Perhaps the most obvious is that countries and regions with the most recorded meteorite falls are also those with the highest population densities (e.g. Europe and Japan); the more people there are to see a meteorite fall the higher the chance of recovering it. The type of meteorite can also play a part (see p.23). Iron meteorites are more likely to be recognized by non-experts and thus are more common among 'find' meteorites. 'Fall' meteorites are dominated by stony meteorites.

Fireballs are much easier to see at night; however, it is much easier to see any associated meteorite land if it is daylight. People may be outside, working or travelling, during the hours of daylight, and therefore there are more potential witnesses to any meteorites falling to the ground. Similarly, seasonal variations in recorded meteorite falls could be explained by the ease (or difficulty) of finding

BELOW World map showing the location of where meteorites have been seen to fall. Note that more meteorites are seen to fall in high population regions, places where there are more people to see a meteorite fall.

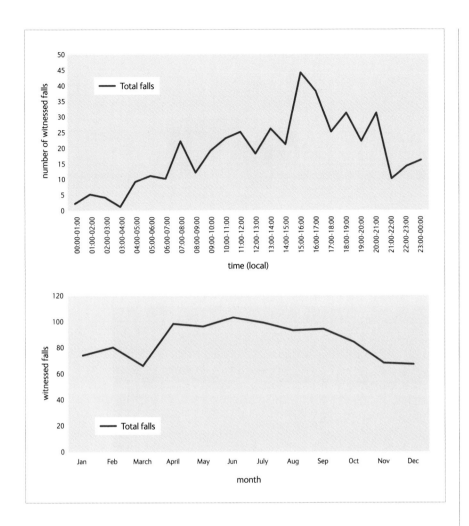

LEFT Graphs showing recorded time of day (upper) and dates of witnessed meteorite falls (lower).

and recovering meteorites. It may be easier to find a meteorite on a frozen lake or in a barren winter field, compared with a highly vegetated area. However, it is likely that more people will be outdoors during spring and summer, so more witnesses are around not only to see a fireball but also to hunt for any potential meteorites. Data seem to indicate that the spring and summer months are advantageous for witnessing meteorite falls.

In an effort to better understand the relationship between meteors, fireballs and meteorites, camera networks dedicated to observing the night sky have been in operation since the 1950s. These cameras have recorded many thousands of meteors and fireballs streaking through the atmosphere and, in a handful of cases, have provided scientists with proof that a meteorite has landed and, more importantly, *where* it has landed.

In addition to providing much more accurate data on how much extraterrestrial material lands on Earth each year, these camera observations have also provided some very important information in our study of meteorites and their place in the solar system. We now have a better understanding of the numbers of meteorites

RIGHT A camera station of the Desert Fireball Network located in the Nullarbor Desert of Western Australia.

RIGHT An image from one of the Desert Fireball Network cameras. A fireball can be seen in the centre-left of the image.

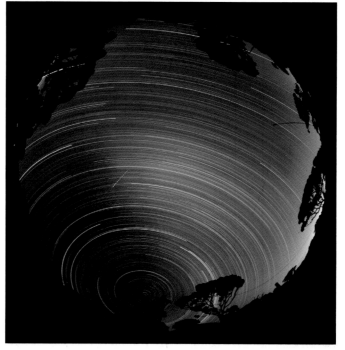

that are arriving on Earth each year. The velocities and trajectories of fireballs have provided scientists with definitive proof that meteorites originate in the solar system. Finally, if the fireball is large enough and if there is sufficient data, it is possible to determine the potential size of any resultant meteorite(s) and also to determine with a fair degree of precision where they will have landed.

Unfortunately, there are only a few camera networks currently in operation around the world that are dedicated to recording fireballs and any resultant meteorite falls: the 'Desert Fireball Network' in south Western Australia, the 'Spanish Meteor Network' and the 'European Fireball Network' in central Europe.

In July 2007, a large fireball was recorded by cameras of the Desert Fireball Network. Not only did calculations indicate that a meteorite landed but it was also possible to determine where the meteorite would be. In late 2008, a search team visited Australia to hunt for the meteorite. Two fragments weighing a total of 324 g (11 ½ oz) were found, only 100 m (328 ft) from the predicted landing site!

Occasionally, large fireballs are witnessed by enough people to enable a large number of accurate eyewitness accounts to be gathered. With security and CCTV cameras becoming more and more common, fireballs may also be recorded on video. The eyewitness accounts and associated video camera footage may be sufficient to calculate the fireball's velocity and trajectory and determine the potential landing site of any resultant meteorite(s).

In the early morning of 24 September 2004, a large fireball was observed to travel over the UK. Over 50 people reported seeing a fireball, from Glasgow in southwest Scotland to towns along the south coast of England, with some reports coming from northern France. Unfortunately, no meteorites were reported to have fallen and it is likely that no material actually survived to reach the ground. However, the eyewitness reports were sufficient for an approximate orbit to

BELOW A still image of the fireball (top left) that produced the Park Forest meteorite, Chicago, USA, taken from a police car video.

BELOW LEFT Map of the UK showing the direction of 24 September 2004 fireball and locations of eye witnesses.

BELOW Schematic diagram showing the orbits of four inner planets and Jupiter, plus the orbits for six recorded meteorites. The orbits of the meteorites were calculated from camera network data and eye-witness accounts.

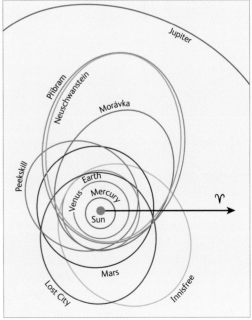

be calculated, which showed that the meteoroid had an orbit typical of a near earth asteroid (see p.39).

Although thousands of meteorites land each year, it is rare to witness a fireball and extremely rare to see a meteorite fall. If you are privileged to witness such an exciting and unique occurrence, there are certain observations you can record that will greatly help scientists investigate the event. Reports of fireball observations can be submitted to meteor and fireball sections of local and/or national astronomical societies. A local university with an astronomy department may also be able to provide you with contact information of where to report your observations.

1 Record the time of day you first saw the fireball/meteorite fall.
2 If you saw a fireball, how long did it last for?
3 How bright was the fireball (compared with the moon, stars or sun), was it coloured, did it have a form or shape?
4 Did the fireball/meteorite leave any form of trail? If so, what did it look like, and how long did it last?
5 What was the direction of the fireball's travel through the sky? This should be related to fixed objects on Earth (e.g. tall buildings) or to star and planet positions in the sky.
6 Did you hear any sound effects? If so, what were they like and when did you hear them?

If you are one of the very rare people fortunate enough to see a meteorite actually land, there are some important things you can record and do.

1 How long after the fall was the meteorite or meteorites recovered?
2 Where was the meteorite(s) found? If possible GPS co-ordinates should be recorded and/or the location marked on a map.
3 How much did the meteorite(s) weigh?
4 What was the ground like where the meteorite landed? Did the meteorite penetrate the ground? If it penetrated the ground, how deep was the hole?

Photographs and drawings of fireballs and any resulting meteorite falls add a huge amount of information and can be extremely useful. Remember if you are entering private property it is vital to gain the landowner's permission. It is also recommended to not touch the meteorite with your bare hands. Meteorites are not dangerous when you pick them up, but they can easily become contaminated with Earth material, which is detrimental to scientific study. Wear gloves and put the meteorite into a clean plastic bag such as a sandwich bag. A suspected meteorite fall should be reported to the nearest large natural history museum, science museum or university geology department. You can find out more about meteorite falls, including examples of 'close encounters' with them, in chapter 3.

METEORITE FINDS

Up to the mid-1960s only about 1,800 meteorites were known, and of these approximately 43% were witnessed falls. As of January 2009, there are roughly 37,000 meteorites known, of which less than 3% are witnessed falls (see the table below). The much greater numbers of meteorites being found today results from the fact that it is now known that certain desert regions of the world are very fertile places to find meteorites. Every year, dedicated collection trips are organized by scientific parties to hot and cold deserts to hunt for meteorites.

KNOWN METEORITES AS OF JANUARY 2009			
	FALLS	FINDS	TOTAL	FALLS AS % OF TOTAL
Stones	1,014	34,769	35,783	2.74
Stony-irons	11	217	228	0.03
Irons	49	934	983	0.13
Total	1,074	35,920	36,994	

ANTARCTICA

The first meteorite recorded to be found in Antarctica was in 1912, during the Australian Antarctica expedition led by Douglas Mawson. Over the next five decades only a handful more meteorites were discovered by various expeditions. It was not thought to be anything unusual to find a few meteorites on this continent; meteorites fall all over the world so why wouldn't they be found in Antarctica?

In 1969, a group of Japanese scientists studying glaciers in Antarctica found nine meteorites near the Yamato Mountains. At first it was thought that these meteorites must have been fragments from a single fall. However, it was soon discovered that they comprised six different meteorite types and, therefore, could not have been from a single meteorite. Continued exploration in the mid- to late 1970s by Japanese teams resulted in many hundreds of meteorites being recovered from this area. After hearing about the amazing meteorite discoveries made by the Japanese, American scientists also started to make dedicated expeditions to Antarctica to hunt for meteorites. The first US expedition in 1976 to the Allan Hills area recovered 11 different meteorites of five different types. Today, in addition to the expeditions run by Japan and the USA, teams of scientists from Europe, China and South Korea all make regular trips to the Antarctic continent to search for meteorites. Up to January 2009, these collecting trips have resulted in over 25,000 meteorites, more than from any other place in the world.

So, why is Antarctica such a good place to find meteorites? Firstly, not only is the Antarctic plateau the coldest place on Earth, it is also the driest place. Any meteorites that land in Antarctica are very likely to be preserved in the dry, deep-freeze conditions, for hundreds of thousands or even millions of years. Secondly,

RIGHT Blue ice moraine of the Dominion Range in Antarctica showing a meteorite collection area. A moraine is a place where a jumble of rocks is left behind from a moving glacier. The rocks in this image are mostly from Earth. Finding meteorites in areas like this takes hard work and is very rewarding.

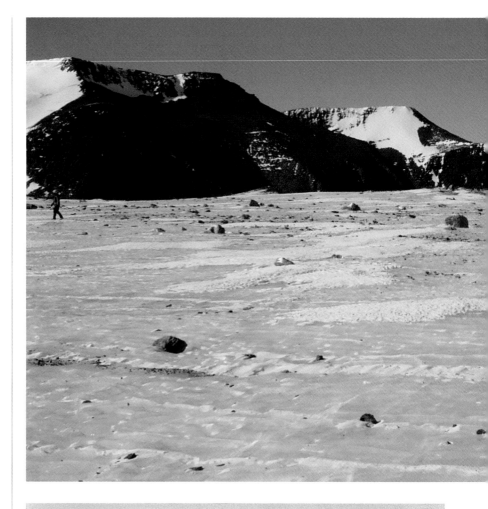

RIGHT Diagram to show how meteorites may be concentrated in certain parts of Antarctica. As glaciers move towards the ocean they carry the meteorites with them. But if their path is blocked, the ice is stripped away by the wind exposing the residue of meteorites.

meteorite fall

wind

area of ice ablation

area of ice accumulation

mountain

bedrock

ABOVE A meteorite on the ice in Antarctica. The dark meteorites are easy to spot against the icy background.

BELOW A satellite image showing the blue-ice fields in the Yamato Mountains region of Antarctica. Blue-ice fields have proven particularly fertile meteorite hunting grounds.

meteorites in Antarctica can be very easy to spot. In areas where there are no other sources of rocks, the only dark objects to be found on the ice are likely to be meteorites. Finally, the movement of the ice concentrates meteorites in some locations. As the ice moves away from the South Pole towards the oceans its movement becomes blocked by mountains (such as the Transantarctic Mountain range), forcing it into confined areas or 'cul de sacs'. Here the strong Antarctic winds (known as katabatic winds) erode or ablate ice from the surface, leaving a residue of rocks that were carried within it. This process concentrates any rocks (including meteorites) that are carried in the ice. The regions where ablation occurs are known as 'blue ice', as the ice has a pale, bluish tinge. Satellite imaging can detect these blue ice regions and so provide scientists with new areas in which to hunt for meteorites. Under the Antarctic Treaty signed in 1961, exploration in Antarctica cannot be used for mining and financial gain. All geological samples from the continent can only be used for scientific study. Therefore, all Antarctic meteorites recovered after the Treaty was signed are kept within scientific institutions and cannot be bought or sold.

HOT DESERTS

Hot desert areas are also favourable places for meteorite preservation, although unlike Antarctica there are no natural processes involved that concentrate the meteorites in specific areas. As of January 2009, more than 8,000 authenticated meteorites have been recovered from hot desert regions around the world. Parts of the Sahara Desert in Libya and the deserts of Oman have proved particularly fruitful for meteorite searches. Meteorites have also been recovered from other desert regions around the world including the Nullarbor Plain in south Western Australia, the Namib Desert in southwestern Africa and the Atacama Desert in Chile.

The very dry conditions in the hot deserts limit the amount of weathering and rusting of the meteorites and so enhance their preservation. The best places to look for meteorites in the hot desert are areas where the ground is flat, where there are few or no dark local rocks that could be mistaken for meteorites, and where there are no sand dunes to cover up any meteorites. However, perhaps most importantly, the area must have remained arid and unchanged for many thousands of years so that the number of meteorites 'builds up' over time. For example, the Nullarbor Plain has been a desert for over 30,000 years.

Hot desert meteorites are found in the place where they landed, and even in a particularly fruitful area you would be lucky to find two or three meteorites in a square kilometre. Of course, some areas have abundant meteorites where tens or even hundreds of samples may be found in a relatively small area of a few square kilometres.

RIGHT A 294 g (10 oz) partially fusion crusted stone from the Camel Donga eucrite strewn field. The orange/brown staining on the black, fusion crusted surface is staining from the local soil.

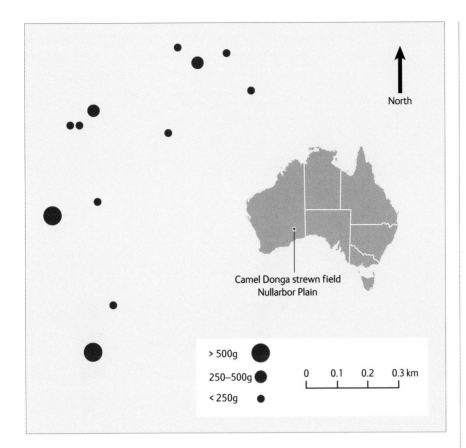

North

Camel Donga strewn field
Nullarbor Plain

> 500g
250–500g
< 250g

0   0.1   0.2   0.3 km

LEFT Map showing sites of finds of stone from the Camel Donga meteorite.

However, these 'strewn fields' are caused as a result of a single meteorite breaking up during flight and producing a shower of stones over a limited area. A well-known site in the Nullarbor Plain is the Camel Donga strewn field, where several hundred fragments (weighing over 25 kg or 62 lb) of a eucrite meteorite have been collected.

In contrast to Antarctica, it is sometimes legal to buy or sell meteorites from hot deserts, or indeed some other locations where they may have been found. However, some countries like Oman and Australia do have strict laws, which restrict the commercial exploitation and export of meteorites. If you are interested in purchasing a meteorite you should make sure that the meteorite has not been illegally exported from its country of origin.

IMPACTS AND COLLISIONS

ALONG .WITH HEATING AND MELTING, impact and collision are fundamental processes in the evolution of the solar system from its formation to the present. Collision is responsible for several effects in the solar system. Impacts at low energies (which mainly took place early on) caused dust-sized particles to stick together to form bigger and bigger bodies like asteroids and planetesimals and, ultimately, planets. As these small bodies collided and bounced into and off each other, the bits and pieces left over started speeding up and soon were causing much more destructive collisions. Impacts at higher energies have altered planetary surfaces such as forming the moon and craters, and causing some planets such as Venus to tilt on their axis. Impacts continue to occur today, although the frequency is much less. In this chapter, we discuss the evidence for impacts, how they have affected the solar system in the past, and the hazard they present today.

OPPOSITE Barringer (or Meteor) Crater in Arizona, USA, is approximately 1.2 km (¾ mile) across and was produced by an impactor about 50 m (164 ft) wide. The remains of the impactor are known as the Canyon Diablo iron meteorite.

EVIDENCE OF IMPACTS

The most obvious effect of impact is a crater. The evidence for impacts in the solar system is not difficult to find. Just look at any of the rocky, inner solar system planets of Mercury, Venus, Earth and Mars, and the moon for confirmation of a very violent history. It is easiest to see the effects on planets that have not been geologically active for billions of years. Mars and Mercury, and also the moon, reveal evidence that these bodies were bombarded quite heavily over time.

BELOW LEFT These craters are on Mercury. The field of view is approximately 160 km (100 miles).

BELOW CENTRE This crater on Mars has formed on a flat surface, and has expanded in a circular fashion. Because of the topography of the impact site, the shape of the crater was disturbed by the walls of the plateau and resulted in an asymmetrical shape.

BELOW RIGHT Impact craters on the moon; Glushko crater has a diameter of 43 km (26 ¾ miles).

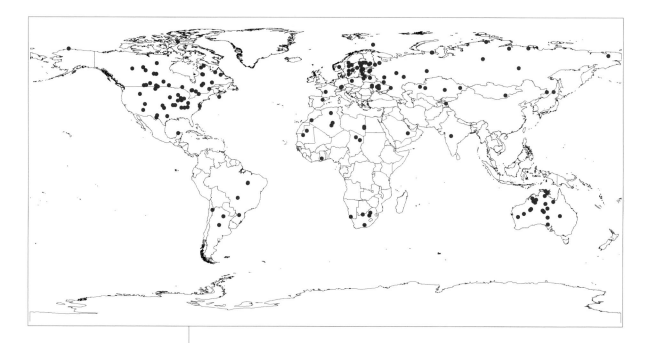

The Earth has also been bombarded throughout its history, but geological processes such as volcanism, and weathering processes have erased or obscured many craters. Currently, there are 180 well-characterised meteorite craters scattered across the Earth's surface. Most are found on the oldest, continental regions (called cratons) that have been stable for billions of years. The largest craters – at Vredefort in South Africa (300 km (186 miles) in diameter) and Sudbury in Canada (250 km (155 miles) across) – are also the oldest, at about 2,000 million years and 1,850 million years, respectively. There is no correlation between age and crater diameter; for example, the Chicxulub crater in the Yucatan is 180 km (112 miles) in diameter and is 65 million years old. Older craters like these are often extensively eroded and are identified through recognition of shock-produced features in the bedrock (see opposite).

CRATERS

Fast-moving meteorites form craters by impacting the Earth's surface so hard that they explode and excavate material. The 50,000-year-old Barringer Crater, also known as Meteor Crater, in Arizona, which is over 1 km (½ mile) across and about 200 m (656 ft) deep, was made by an iron meteorite approximately 50 m (164 ft) in diameter. An object of this diameter would weigh about 300,000 t. Over 30 t of an iron meteorite, known as Canyon Diablo, have been collected around Barringer Crater, accounting for approximately 0.01% of the mass of the impactor. The remaining material vaporized on impact. Some of this material is now found as small, metallic spherules in the soil around the crater. Fortunately, impacts of this magnitude occur only every 20,000 years or so, but, with the spread and speed of growth of population centres, and increasing urbanization of the landscape, humanity is more and more likely to suffer a catastrophic cosmic impact.

The mechanism behind crater formation is the reaction of rock to compression and decompression during shock. At impact, a shock wave moves forwards into the rock that has been hit and also backwards into the impactor, melting and vaporizing it. The high shock pressures compress the rocks. A decompression front follows the pressure wave that allows the shocked material to be ejected outwards in a sheet of material. The walls of the newly forming crater are lined with material vaporized from the impactor and the impact site. The floor of the crater consists of broken up and glassy material, rocks that have been distorted or melted during impact. They contain remnants of the impactor.

Simple craters (of which Meteor Crater is an excellent example), are less than 3-4 km (1 ¾ - 2 ½ miles) across. They are bowl-shaped, almost always circular depressions, and are formed by impactors less than 1 km (²/₃ mile) across. Larger impactors produce more complex craters, many kilometres across. Complex craters may have a central uplift, or plateau, produced as the shocked, unexcavated strata rebound from the impact, similar to water droplets on a pond rebounding and producing an initially raised central

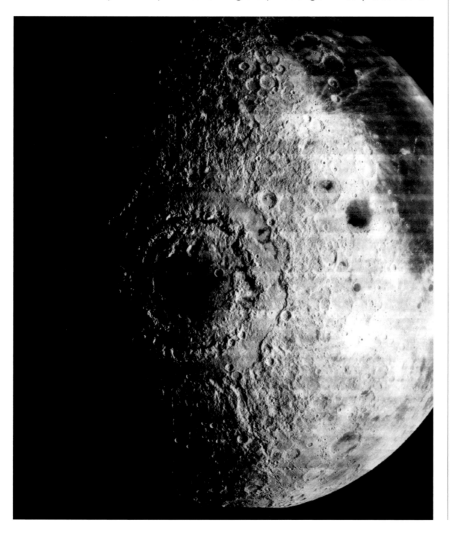

LEFT The Mare Orientale basin on the moon, taken by Luna Orbiter 4. The multi-ringed basin is about 300 km (186 miles) across and was formed by a giant impact early in the moon's history.

point from which ripples radiate. They are sometimes multi-ringed, the rings caused by slumping of the crater walls. The crater floor is often filled with a thick layer of shock-melted glass, or impact melt, which contains trace remnants of the impactor. Some of the most spectacular complex craters, or multi-ringed basins, are seen on the moon.

Not all meteorite impacts with Earth generate craters. Sometimes, a meteorite might have enough mass, but it breaks into smaller bits as it burns up in the atmosphere. These smaller pieces reach terminal velocity (also known as free fall velocity) more rapidly, and these meteorites will 'bump' into the Earth with enough force to leave a dent, but not enough energy to form the characteristic features of a crater such as shock-produced minerals or overturning of materials. In 2007, a meteorite crashed into the Earth in Peru, leaving a hole about 15 m (49 ft) in diameter and 5 m (16 ½ ft) in depth.

A spectacular example of a meteorite that broke up in the atmosphere is the Park Forest meteorite that fell near Chicago, Illinois, in 2003. This meteorite is estimated to have weighed thousands of kilograms before entering Earth's atmosphere, but it broke up into smaller pieces, the largest of which was just over 5 kg (11 lb). This meteorite formed no crater.

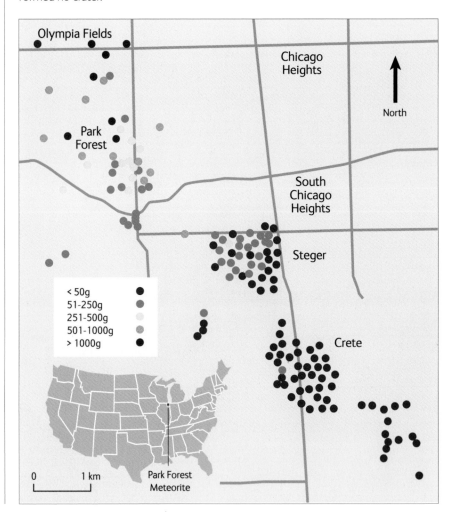

RIGHT Map of the Park Forest, Chicago, USA suburban area showing the locations where fragments of the Park Forest meteorite were found.

THE TUNGUSKA IMPACT EVENT

Early in the morning of 30 June 1908, a very bright fireball was visible over the remote Tunguska region of Siberia. Contemporary reports record that explosions like thunder were heard. In Russia, Germany and the UK, seismographs recorded tremors, and barographs recorded air pressure waves at the time of the explosions. It was not until almost 20 years later in 1927, that the Russian scientist Leonid Kulik led an expedition to the region to search for the remnants of what was presumed to have been a meteorite impact. Kulik did not find a meteorite crater, but an area of devastation about 60 km (37 miles) across. A belt of dead trees that appeared to have been blasted in an intense forest fire surrounded an approximately circular area of swamp. Alignment of the trees, pointing radially outward from the swamp, suggested that they had been felled by a shock wave. Only small particles of meteoritic material have been found in peat and tree resin in the area. It is assumed that an impactor (possibly 50 m (164 ft) across) exploded 6–8 km (3 ¾-5 miles) up in the atmosphere and the heat and shock wave from the explosion burnt and blew down the trees. It is still not certain whether the impactor was a comet or an asteroid. The energy of the impact has been estimated as 10^{17}J (equivalent to 50 million tonnes of TNT).

BELOW Part of the devastated region of Tunguska in Siberia photographed during the 1927 expedition to the area.

ABOVE Aerial view of the New Quebec impact crater with its 250-m (820-ft) deep lake. The crater is about 3.4 km (2 miles) across and formed about 1.4 million years ago.

SHOCK FEATURES

Recognition of craters is often very easy: the bowl-shaped depression of Barringer Crater in Arizona is unmistakable. However, this crater is, geologically speaking, a very young crater in a semi-desert landscape. Craters that formed millions of years ago might be buried by sediments, eroded, or otherwise obscured or erased. The shape of the landscape is therefore usually insufficient to recognise a crater, although aerial photography can be used to find rounded features that can be investigated in more detail.

There are features preserved in impacted rocks that record the impact shock. These include microscopic signs, such as the presence of different forms of a mineral (e.g. stishovite and coesite, which are shock-produced forms of quartz), or deformation features within a mineral. The occurrence of microtektites (melted beads of glass) and tiny diamonds, formed from carbon as the result of the intense shock pressures, also indicate shock processing.

LEFT Magnified view of quartz crystals showing deformation features. The field of view is about 0.5 mm (¹⁄₅₀ in) across.

0.5 mm

LEFT Stereomicroscopic view of microtektites (the three pale-yellow, transparent glass spherules amongst the host detritus) collected from the tops of various Victoria Land Transantarctic Mountains, Antarctica.

ABOVE Shatter cones in rocks associated with the Vredefort impact structure in South Africa. The pen is about 12.7 cm (5 in) long.

Another feature that can be used to determine an impact origin is the presence of shatter cones. These are cone-shaped fragments of rock that form as a result of the high velocity and pressure of the shock wave produced by the impact. They can be seen in rock exposures that might have been several kilometres away from the impact origin. The apex of the shatter cone always points to the centre of the impact, and thus mapping the distribution and orientation of shatter cones can help define an impact site.

IMPACT RATES

The amount of extraterrestrial material that falls on the Earth each year has been estimated at between 40,000 and 60,000 t. Almost all of this material arrives as dust grains much less than 1 mm (^{1}/$_{25}$ in) across – about two particles per square kilometre per second hit the Earth. Larger bodies impact less frequently, fewer than 40 meteorites weighing over 100 kg (220 lb) fall each year. Although this may seem like a large mass, it takes an object weighing a minimum of 50,000 kg (110,231 lb) to make a crater. Because much of the Earth's surface is covered by water, or is uninhabited, most of these meteorites fall unobserved. Only about a dozen are seen to fall each year.

One way of calculating a cratering rate for the Earth is to use the number and ages of craters on the moon. Since the moon is so close to the Earth, the cratering rate of Earth and moon is likely to have been similar. But the moon is a geologically inactive, airless body (it has no atmosphere to protect it from impactors by slowing them down), and so craters on its surface have been less modified through time than those on the Earth. Based on lunar craters and terrestrial continental craters, the rate at which craters with diameters greater than 10 km (6 miles) are formed on Earth is estimated at less than four craters per million years. The rate is thought to be lower now than in the earliest epoch of Earth's history, when the inner solar system had not been fully cleared of the debris remaining from planetary formation.

As the size of a meteorite increases, the smaller the number that fall each year, but the greater the potential impact hazard. Based on records of meteorite falls over the last 200 years combined with theoretical modelling results, two meteorites weighing about 1,000 kg (2204 lb) are expected to fall roughly every year, and one weighing about 100,000 kg or 1 t (220,462 lb) every 100 years or so.

The biggest meteorite to fall in recent times landed in thick forest in the Sikhote-Alin mountains in Russia, in February 1947. Approximately 23 t of material was recovered at the time and at least a further 4 t has been unearthed subsequently. The fall was accompanied by a spectacular shower of fireballs, which made over 100 impact holes in the ground, the largest of which was almost 30 m (98 ½ ft) in diameter.

LEFT A stamp issued in 1957 to commemorate the fall of the Sikhote-Alin meteorite in 1947.

BELOW This young boy was lucky to escape serious injury when the Mbale meteorite fell in 1992.

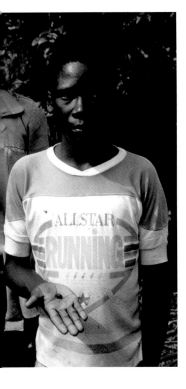

HAZARDS FROM IMPACTS AND COLLISIONS

The impact hazard from the fall of a meteorite in the 1–10 kg (2 ¼-22 lb) size range is minimal. A person receiving a direct hit would probably die, and yet there are no well-documented instances of human fatality from a local meteorite impact. The most widely reported injuries associated with impact are those of a young boy in Mbale, Uganda, and a woman in Sylacauga, Alabama, USA. In August 1992, the boy was playing football with his friends, when a shower of about 50 stones fell. The stones ranged in size from 0.1 g to 27.4 kg (3/100-60 ½ lb), and the boy was hit on the head by one of the smaller stones, weighing approximately 3 g (¹/₁₀ oz). He escaped with bruises rather than any more serious injuries because the fall of the

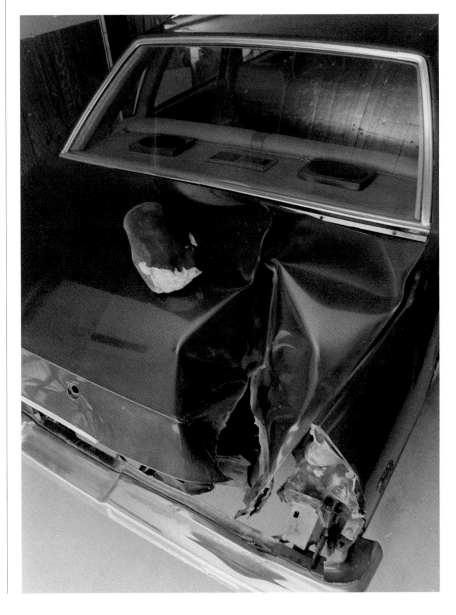

RIGHT The Peekskill meteorite, and the car that it hit when it fell in October 1992.

stone had been broken by the leaves of a banana tree. In November 1954, a woman was resting in her home in Sylacauga, Alabama, USA when a piece of 5 kg (11 lb) meteorite crashed through the roof of her house and struck her on the hip. She had a large bruise but no other physical injuries.

There have been many instances of buildings and parked cars being hit by meteorites. The meteorite that fell in Benld, Illinois, in 1938 managed to hit both a building and a car, as it fell through the roof of a garage and into the car parked inside. After passing through the floor of the car, the meteorite bounced back and finally embedded itself in the back seat. More recently, in the early evening of 9 October 1992, a stone meteorite fell onto a Chevrolet parked in Peekskill, New York. The Peekskill meteoroid was accompanied by a bright fireball (see p.9) that was observed and recorded as it travelled across the northeastern USA, before landing in the boot (or trunk) of the car (see opposite).

The main hazard to the Earth is posed by the so-called near earth objects (NEOs). These are asteroids and comets that have orbits that bring them to within 45,000,000 km (27,961,704 miles) of the Earth's orbit.

LEFT Diagram of the inner solar system illustrating the orbits of the main belt asteroids and the near Earth asteroid groups – the Amors, Atens and Apollos.

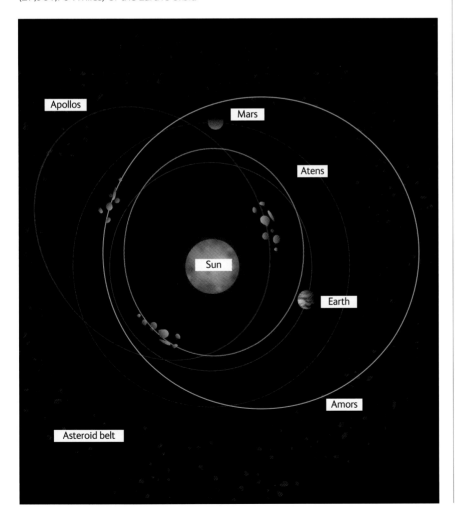

THE CRETACEOUS–TERTIARY BOUNDARY EVENT

Approximately 65 million years ago, at the end of the Cretaceous period, there was a dramatic drop in the numbers of species present on the Earth. This mass extinction has been linked with the collision of a huge meteorite with the Earth. The impact site was at Chicxulub in the Yucatan Peninsula in the Gulf of Mexico. The crater is now buried, but geophysical surveys estimate its diameter to be roughly 180 km (112 miles).

Environmental effects caused by an impact of these dimensions include massive fires ignited by heat radiated from the impact, and a darkening of the sky due to ejected rock dust and smoke followed by a rapid, global drop in temperature. In the case of Chicxulub, the impact was into sedimentary rock, including sulphate-bearing rocks. This would

have resulted in tonnes of sulphur oxides being ejected into the atmosphere. The energy of the impact, fused nitrogen and oxygen from the atmosphere into nitrogen oxides. As the temperature dropped, sulphur and nitrogen oxides washed out of the atmosphere as acid rain. These consequences affected the entire globe, not just the local region, and for an extended period of time. It is entirely possible that the global environmental changes caused the extinction of many species, including the dinosaurs, although this theory is by no means completely accepted by many palaeontologists.

BELOW Radar topography of the 180 km (112 miles) Chicxulub crater on the Yucatan Peninsula. The dashed line shows the crater rim.

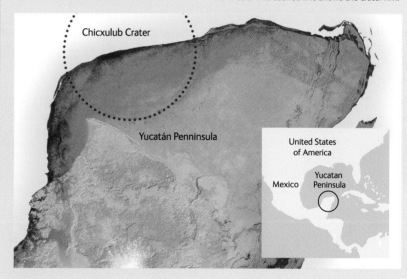

Chicxulub Crater

Yucatán Penninsula

United States of America

Mexico

Yucatan Peninsula

Most asteroids have very well-defined orbits that fall between the orbits of Mars and Jupiter in the asteroid belt, while comets (see chapter 5) have orbits much further from the sun. Sometimes the orbits of these small bodies can be nudged by the massive planets and they can head inwards towards the Earth. Most of the NEOs are asteroids, rather than comets. The asteroids are called near earth asteroids, and they are divided into three groups called the Amor, Aten and Apollo asteroids.

As of January 2009 there were a total of 6,021 NEOs known, of which 1,026 are classified as potentially hazardous. For an object to be classified as potentially hazardous, it must have an orbit that brings it within 750,000 km (466,028 miles) of the Earth's orbit at some point in the future. These are classified as hazardous based only on orbit. Further research must be carried out to determine the size of the body.

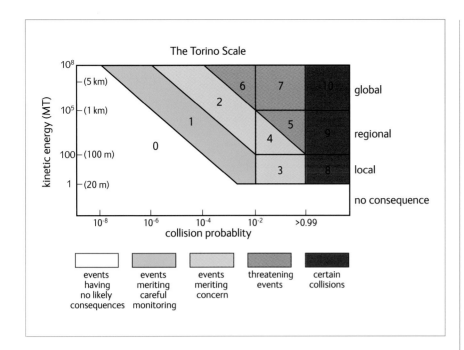

The Torino Scale

LEFT Schematic representation of the Torino Scale established to report the potential hazard of an impacting NEO.

It is now thought that a global catastrophe (which would wipe out humanity) could be triggered by an impact of an asteroid or comet around 1 km (about ½ mile) across. The challenge is to map the orbits of all NEOs down to diameters of around 1 km (about ½ mile). This work is currently being undertaken by several international groups. One of the problems of tracking an NEO is that several observations over multiple orbits must be made before its final orbit is refined. Over the past few years there have been several reported 'near misses'. In order to reduce the danger of 'crying wolf' too frequently, the Torino Scale was devised in 1999. This scale, analogous to the Richter Scale for earthquakes, is used for reporting the potential hazard of NEOs. To date, no hazard greater than 0 on the scale has been reported.

SOURCES AND TYPES OF METEORITES

METEORITES ARRIVE ON EARTH from three well-determined sources. The vast majority (*c.* 97%) of meteorites originate from asteroids, a few meteorites come from the moon (see p.74), and a few from the planet Mars (see p.79). There is evidence to suggest that a very rare type of meteorite may come from comets, but this is still an area of scientific debate (see chapter 5).

The most common class of stone meteorites is the chondrites; these samples are little changed since they formed, early in our solar system's history (see p.47). Other stone meteorites, the achondrites, show signs of melting and recrystallization and record igneous processes on their parent bodies (see p.67). Iron and stony-iron meteorites have also been melted and provide us with insights into the first stages of planet-forming processes (see p.49).

ASTEROIDS AND METEORITES

Stony-iron meteorites, iron meteorites, chondrite meteorites and most of the achondrite meteorites originate from asteroids. Asteroids, or minor planets, are small bodies of rock and metal which are the remains of the first materials to form in our solar system, nearly 4.6 billion years ago. It is a common misconception that asteroids are an 'exploded planet'. In fact, asteroids are bodies that were never part of a single parent planet. The effect of Jupiter's gravity kept the asteroid bodies apart and prevented them from aggregating. It is estimated that there are over one million asteroids greater than 1 km (about ½ mile) in diameter within the asteroid belt. However, if you were to add all the asteroids together, their total mass would be less than that of the moon.

OPPOSITE Microscope image of chondrite showing chondrules, typical of primitive meteorites. Horizontal field of view, 3.3 mm (¹/₁₀ in).
BELOW Photomontage of asteroids Ida (left), about 30 km (19 miles) long x10 km (6 miles) wide, and Gaspra (right), about 17 km (10 ½ miles) long.

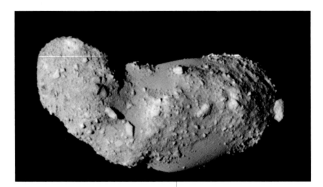

ABOVE Image of the asteroid Itokawa as imaged by the Hyabusa (Japanese) space mission. This is a very small asteroid of about 500 m (1640 ft) long. The surface of the asteroid shows a rubbly texture.

Most asteroids orbit the sun in a belt between the orbits of Mars and Jupiter and they form a boundary between the inner, rocky planets (also known as the terrestrial planets), and the outer, gas and ice-rich planets. These asteroids are known as main belt asteroids. They have roughly circular orbits and have been in stable orbits within the asteroid belt since they formed. However, other asteroids have more elliptical orbits, some of which approach or even cross the orbits of the inner, rocky planets (Mercury, Venus, Mars and Earth) and occasionally they impact these planets' surfaces. Asteroids with orbits that cross that of the Earth's are known as near earth objects (NEOs, see chapter 3).

Geological history records past collisions between asteroids and the rocky planets, and impact craters scar their surfaces. On Earth large impacts are often associated with significant changes in the planet's biodiversity, through extinctions and evolutionary change (see p.40). Space missions that have visited and imaged asteroids, such as the NASA NEAR (Near Earth Asteroid Rendezvous) mission and the Japanese Hayabusa mission, show that asteroids have irregular shapes and

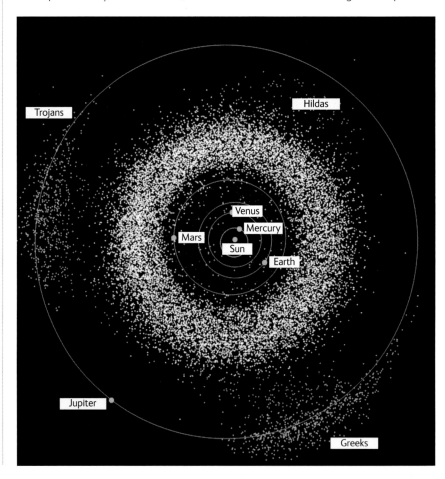

RIGHT Distribution of asteroids in the inner solar system.

their surfaces are highly cratered. This suggests that asteroids have suffered many collisions and impacts during their long lives. These collisions provide the majority of the meteorite material we have on Earth today (see chapter 3).

As we have learned in chapter 2, calculations of the orbits of fireballs that subsequently produced recovered meteorites, provided definitive proof that these meteorites originated in the asteroid belt. Observations of asteroids by telescopes have also provided evidence of the intimate link between asteroids and meteorites.

As is the case with all other solar system bodies, asteroids reflect sunlight from their surfaces. The colours, or spectra, of this reflected light are dependent on the composition of the asteroid. Spectroscopic observations of asteroids by telescopes on Earth, and from spacecraft that have visited asteroids, show that they can be subdivided into different types on the basis of their spectral signatures: rocky, metallic, rock and metal, and carbonaceous. From these basic characteristic spectroscopic signatures, there appear to be at least 14 different asteroid groups.

Asteroids can also be divided into families based on their orbital characteristics. Asteroids in the same families tend to share the same compositions and so they are assumed to have formed through the break-up of a larger, pre-existing asteroid.

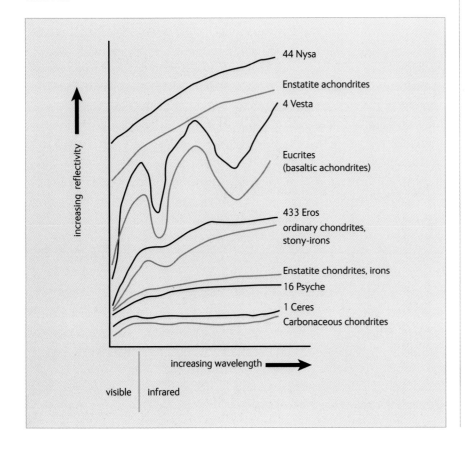

LEFT Spectra of asteroids show some similarities with the measured spectra of meteorites. The strong similarity between the basaltic achondrites (eucrites and also the related howardites and diogenites) suggest that these meteorites were derived from 4 Vesta.

HOW ARE ASTEROIDS NAMED?

When an asteroid is discovered it is given a provisional name. The letter after the year designates the half-month period within the year it was found. 'A' would be for the first half of January, 'B' for the second half, and so on. For instance, the 'E' in 1981 ES4 indicates that it was discovered in the first half of March. The second letter plus the number denote the order of discovery during that half-month period. So for our example above, it was the 118th asteroid observed in that two-week period because 4 x 25 (number of letters in the alphabet minus 'I') + 18 ('S') = 118.

An asteroid is only formally named once its orbit has been confirmed; it is then given a number, according to the date when the data on its orbit were determined. Finally, a name can be assigned. For example (4) Vesta is the 4th asteroid discovered, while (9007) James Bond is the 9,007th asteroid discovered. Although there are over 200,000 asteroids with numbers, less than 20,000 have been given names. The choice of name is up to the discoverer(s); however, it is convention that NEOs are still given traditional names whereas main belt asteroids are often named after individuals, some of whom may (or may not) be famous. Once a name has been chosen by the discoverer(s) the International Astronomical Union votes to accept and publish the names.

Asteroids have been named after musicians, such as (1034) Mozartia and (1815) Beethoven, as well as (4147) Lennon, (4148) McCartney, (4149) Harrison and (4150) Starr; artists including (6676) Monet and (4511) Rembrandt; writers such as (2985) Shakespeare and (3047) Goethe; scientists such as (697) Galilea, (662) Newtonia, (8000) Isaac Newton, (1991) Darwin and (2001) Einstein; plus other miscellaneous people such as (5497) Sararussell, (6579) Benedix and (4259) McCoy.

Scientists can also compare spectroscopic data from asteroids with those of meteorites on the Earth. There are good matches between some meteorite classes and some asteroid types. The howardite, eucrite and diogenite (HED) group of meteorites (see p.69) have similarities in their chemistries, suggesting that they formed in the same asteroid. Spectral studies of the HEDs show a very strong match with one of the largest asteroids known, 4 Vesta. It seems very likely that these meteorites are derived either from this asteroid or perhaps from the 'Vestoids' – asteroids that are believed to have originally been part of 4 Vesta, which were ejected from its south pole region in a very large impact.

However, there are also inconsistencies between the distribution of asteroid types and the classes of meteorites. For example, the most abundant asteroid type (spectral class C) has very similar spectral characteristics to the stony, carbonaceous chondrite meteorites. However, the carbonaceous chondrites are not particularly abundant on Earth, representing only around 3% of known meteorites. The most common type of meteorite, the ordinary chondrites (c. 85% of all known meteorites), do not have a clear spectral match with any known asteroid. The inconsistencies in the spectra of known meteorite classes, with the spectra of asteroids, suggest that meteorites originate from asteroids that are not typical of the total asteroid population. To put it another way, the meteorites we have on Earth are not representative samples of the asteroids. It is estimated that all the meteorites on Earth originated from around 100 parent asteroids. This represents just a tiny fraction of the asteroid belt.

UNMELTED METEORITES AND PLANET FORMATION

Meteorites are divided into three main types: stones, irons and stony-irons, as discussed on p.7. Stony meteorites are further subdivided into the unmelted chondrites and the melted achondrites.

CHONDRITES

Chondrites are thought to have formed at the same time and from the same material as the inner rocky planets of our solar system. Studying them can tell us about how the planets were made and about the materials that originally formed our own planet. They are a jumbled mixture of materials that date from the time that the solar system formed. Most of the components are usually a few millimetres across or smaller. The major constituents are chondrules – rounded, millimetre-sized, once-molten objects that formed during a fast-heating event. (Chondrules are named from the Greek word 'chondros', meaning 'seed' or 'little grain'.) Chondrites also contain shiny flecks of iron-nickel metal, plus occasionally pale-coloured patches of calcium and aluminium-rich inclusions (CAIs). The fine-grained matrix surrounding these objects is made up of fragments of chondrules, along with organic material and ancient pre-solar grains (see p.57).

Chondrites are divided into four main classes: ordinary (O), carbonaceous (C), enstatite (E) and rumuruti (R) chondrites. These four types may have formed at different distances from the sun. Ordinary chondrites, as the name implies, are

ABOVE The Ivuna carbonaceous chondrite. This type of meteorite is the richest in volatile elements.

LEFT The Parnallee ordinary chondrite, containing many chondrules.

RIGHT Except for gases such as hydrogen and helium, the chemical composition of carbonaceous chondrites such as Ivuna and the sun is very similar.

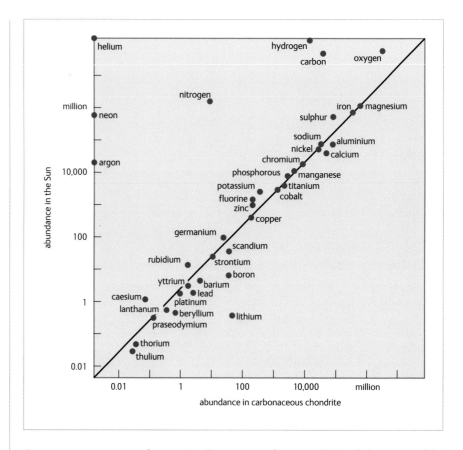

the most common type of meteorite. They account for around 90% of all meteorite falls. Carbonaceous chondrites are much less common, but perhaps can tell us even more about the origins of the solar system. They have a composition that is richer in volatile substances (such as carbon-bearing compounds) than the ordinary chondrites. In fact, the composition of some of them is extremely similar to that of the sun, minus the gaseous hydrogen and helium that make up the vast majority of solar material. For this reason they are thought to represent the composition of the inner planets within the solar system, and their composition is used by geochemists to compare to terrestrial rocks.

Enstatite chondrites are notable for having very oxygen-poor compositions, so much so that elements that usually bond with oxygen in other meteorites (and on Earth) have formed compounds with sulphur. Rumuruti chondrites, in contrast, have more oxygen for bonding than the other meteorite groups and, thus, are devoid of metal. In addition to the four main types of chondrite, there are also several chondrites that do not fit very well into any of the known groups.

As well as differing in chemistry, the different chondrite groups can be distinguished by their oxygen isotopes. Oxygen has three isotopes: oxygen-16 (the most abundant), oxygen-17 and oxygen-18. The proportion of these isotopes is dependent on different factors, such as how much alteration by heat or water the meteorite has suffered, and so the oxygen isotopic compositions varies between meteorites. This variation is an important tool used in meteorite classification.

FORMATION OF THE SOLAR SYSTEM

1 A turbulent cloud of interstellar dust and gas collapses.
2 The dust and gas cloud forms a spinning disc.
3 The temperature and pressure of the disc increases towards the middle. Eventually, the temperature in the centre is hot enough for fusion of hydrogen into helium to begin. The central star is born.
4 The remaining dust and gas clump together, gradually sweeping up all the debris into planets.

PLANET FORMATION

The mechanism by which planets formed can be investigated in three ways: by looking at rocks that formed very early in our solar system's history, such as chondrites; by observing young stars to look for signs of planet formation; and by theoretical models of planet formation. All three approaches have contributed to what we know of our planet's origins. To understand what meteorites can tell us about the formation of the planets, we must first look to theoretical and observational information about planet formation.

A HISTORY OF PLANET FORMATION THEORIES Since Copernicus' discovery that the planets orbit the sun, there have been three major theories about how the planets formed. One of the most popular theories, first postulated by the astronomer James Jeans (1877–1946), was the ejection hypothesis. This states that the material

ABOVE Young stars imaged using new-generation telescopes provide clues about the origins of our own sun and solar system, and show how the planets may have formed from a dusty disc surrounding the young sun.

planets were formed from, was ejected from the sun as a filament of gas following a collision with a giant comet or another star. The theory was later rejected because planets are relatively enriched in the hydrogen isotope, deuterium, and the element lithium, which would be destroyed in a star. A second major theory, developed in the 1930s, was the capture hypothesis, which states that passing material was captured by the early sun's gravitational pull. Although the capture hypothesis has never been disproved, recent astronomical observations make the third, and oldest theory – the nebula hypothesis – more attractive. By the nebula theory, the solar system formed from a rotating, flattened disc. This idea was first proposed by the Prussian philosopher and astronomer Immanuel Kant in 1755, and further developed by Pierre-Simon, Marquis de Laplace, in 1796. It remains the most widely accepted theory of planet formation to this day, because it is compatible with both the observational astronomical evidence and evidence from meteorites.

The modern-day nebula theory pictures the sun and planets forming at the same time, from the same dense cloud of interstellar dust and gas. As most of the cloud, collapsed by gravity, swirled inwards to form the sun, the remains of the infalling cloud began to form a rotating disc, called an accretion disc or solar nebula, around the central star, from which the planets were born.

OBSERVATIONAL EVIDENCE: PROTOPLANETARY AND DEBRIS DISCS

Most very young stars, less than about 5 million years old, have discs of dust and gas, called protoplanetary discs. These discs become less and less common around progressively older stars, as they dissipate or form planets. The dust is mainly a mix of silicates, carbonaceous material and ices, much like our own solar system at the time of its formation, and the gas is mostly hydrogen and helium.

Around 15% of nearby older stars also have discs around them. These discs have proportionally large amounts of dust and small amounts of gas. One of the best-known examples is Beta Pictoris. Since dust is expected to fall into the star over a short timescale, these dusty discs around old stars are probably continually replenished with new dust from asteroids and comets. Some of the discs are ring-shaped, with a hole close to the star. What is in the hole? Paradoxically, telescopes enable us to detect large clouds of the tiny dust grains, even though at the same range individual planets, asteroids and comets remain invisible to us. The inner holes could be full of planets. In fact, our own solar system, if viewed from a neighbouring star, would also look like a star surrounded by empty space in place of the planets, but clearly showing the dust ring beyond Neptune (this dust ring is known as the Kuiper Belt and is described in more detail in chapter 5).

Recent advances in telescopes are finally allowing us to see planets around other stars. It seems our suspicions that many dusty discs go on to form planetary systems is correct. Many mature stars appear to have one or more planets orbiting around them.

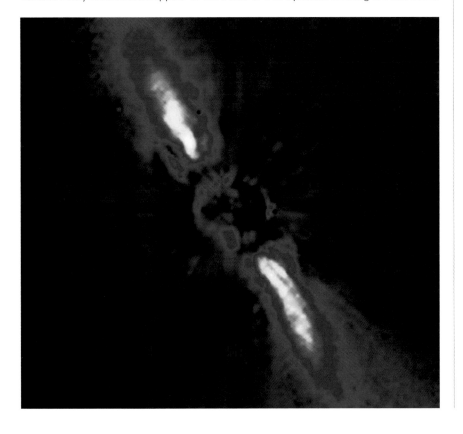

LEFT Telescope image of dusty disc around the star Beta Pictoris.

FORMATION OF THE TERRESTRIAL PLANETS: THE STORY FROM METEORITES Much of our knowledge about the formation of the terrestrial planets, the four inner, rocky planets, comes from meteorites. Meteorites reveal a complex picture of planet growth. The first stage is the coagulation of dust grains, which are initially only a millionth of a metre across or less. Dust coagulation was aided by heating events that allowed the dust to melt and stick together to make chondrules. These objects then collided, and perhaps because they were moving at such gentle relative speeds that they could accrete, or using organic material as glue, formed metre to kilometre-sized boulders, called planetesimals. Once the planetesimals reached a certain size, greater than a kilometre or so, they began to have a significant gravitational field. This made their growth much easier and quicker, as other planetesimals were attracted to them and their growth progressed by impacts of these relatively large bodies. This stage is called 'runaway growth'. Although this broad outline of how planets formed seems to fit most of the features seen in meteorites, deciphering the history recorded in meteorites to understand the details of planet formation proves much more difficult. Some important questions remain. How exactly did chondrules form? What was the heat source for early planets? How long did the process of planet formation take? Ongoing studies of meteorites are helping to address these questions.

RIGHT Microscope image of a radial pyroxene chondrule from the ALH 88036 (H3.4) ordinary chondrite. The chondrule is about 2 mm (1/12 in) across.

BELOW Different types of chondrules

TOP, ABOVE AND LEFT Microscope images of a porphyritic olivine and pyroxene chondrule from the Palmyra (L3) ordinary chondrite (the chondrule is about 1.8 mm or 7/100 in across); barred olivine chondrule from the Palmyra ordinary chondrite (the chondrule is about 1.2 mm or 4/100 in across); the textures of different chondrule types in the Etihudna (L4) ordinary chondrite (field of view 4 mm or 1/4 in).

COMPONENTS OF CHONDRITES

CHONDRULES These are near-spherical, typically millimetre-sized stony objects, which probably formed by a sudden, flash heating event at temperatures of over 1,400°C (2,552°F) followed by fast cooling, and solidification of the resulting molten droplets. Chondrules are mostly made up of the magnesium, iron, silicon and oxygen-rich minerals olivine and pyroxene. The exact details of the process and the nature of the heat source that produced these objects early in solar system history are some of the long-standing mysteries in meteoritics. It is important to find the answers to these questions, since this tells us how the very first stage of planet formation, the accretion of tiny dust particles into larger millimetre to centimetre-sized balls, took place. By looking at the chemistry and texture of chondrules we can place a few constraints on how they formed. For example, many chondrules appear to contain 'chondrules within chondrules', suggesting that they experienced a high-temperature heating event more than once. The main theories for chondrule formation involve a shock wave in the early solar system, a jet from the sun, or collision between planetesimals, and these theories are discussed further below.

The shock-wave theory argues that in the early solar system there would have been waves of high pressure passing through the inner region where the planets and asteroids formed. The shock of being hit by this wave of pressure would be enough to heat and melt dustballs and cause them to form chondrules. The second theory argues that the chondrules formed extremely close to the sun. Particles spiralled inwards towards the early sun, and most material ended up flowing into the growing

BELOW These images show changes over only a five-year period in the disc and jets of this newborn star, which is about half a million years old. The young stars are obscured by a dark disc of dust. Because of changes in the local magnetic field, violent jets of material are ejected from near to the central star.

200 A.U.

1995   1998   2000

sun. However, changes in the magnetic field around the sun caused material to rise up in big jets. As the grains were lifted, they were exposed to the full intensity of the sunlight, which heated them up and caused chondrules to form. The jets then deposited the chondrules onto the dusty disc around the sun at the distance that the asteroids and planets were forming. Evidence for this process is found in observational astronomy – young stars are observed to have jets streaming out. One of the main lines of evidence for the third theory, planetesimal collisions, is that some chondrites contain rare rock fragments that have undergone melting themselves. It is argued that these rock fragments came from planets that must have existed before the chondrites formed. Chondrules may then have formed as a product of high-energy collisions between planetesimals just tens or hundreds of kilometres in diameter. In truth, all three (or more) processes may have formed chondrules, and the challenge for us now is to understand which were most important.

METAL One thing that best distinguishes chondrites from terrestrial rock is that they almost always contain flecks of metal – a mixture of iron and nickel. This makes chondrites slightly attracted to a magnet, and provides a good test for meteorites. The presence of metal within the stony matrix is extremely important. It implies that the rock has not been melted since the earliest times in the solar system, because the molten metal has not sunk to the core of its parent asteroid, as has happened on Earth. The quantity of metal in chondrites is quite variable, from 2% to 20%, and metal content provides an important means of classifying chondrites of different types.

BELOW The Beddgelert (H5) ordinary chondrite clearly showing flecks of iron-nickel metal.

RIGHT The Allende carbonaceous chondrite, partly covered in jet-black fusion crust. This contains numerous white inclusions called CAIs. This stone is about 10 cm (4 in) across.

BELOW A CAI from the Leoville carbonaceous chondrite. It is 2 cm (¾ in) across.

CAIS In February 1969 a large shower of stony meteorites fell near the village of Pueblito de Allende, Mexico. The meteorite turned out to be of the rare carbonaceous chondrite variety. Many of these stones were quickly retrieved and over 2 t of material was collected and eagerly studied by meteorite scientists all over the world. One immediately obvious and unusual feature of the Allende meteorite is that on each surface millimetre to centimetre-sized, irregularly shaped, pale-coloured inclusions are clearly visible. These are calcium and aluminium-rich inclusions (CAIs).

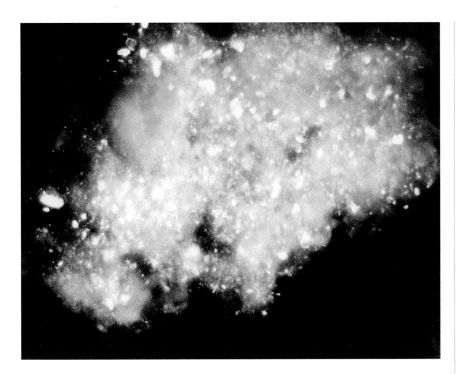

LEFT A cluster of millions of diamonds, separated from the Allende meteorite. Some scientists believe these are pre-solar.

CAIs have a composition that is subtly different to chondrules; they are typically much more enriched in the high-temperature elements calcium and aluminium, and contain less abundant silicon, magnesium, iron and more-volatile substances. The ages of several CAIs have been measured and they have been found to be the oldest known solids in the solar system, dating from around 4,568 million years ago. They are quite common in carbonaceous chondrites, but extremely rare in ordinary and enstatite chondrites. They are also different from chondrules in their oxygen isotope composition. The formation mechanism of CAIs is unknown, but it may be similar to that of chondrules, although CAIs seem to have been heated for longer, and cooled more slowly. An important difference between the two types of objects is that not all CAIs formed from molten droplets. A few CAIs have fragile, intricate textures like snowflakes, suggesting that they condensed directly from a vapour to a solid without ever being molten.

PRE-SOLAR GRAINS The matrix of chondritic meteorites contains some tiny crystals of very resilient minerals, such as diamond, silicon carbide, corundum, silicon nitride and graphite. The isotopic composition of these grains is completely different to the composition of everything else in their host meteorites, or indeed anything on Earth or in the rest of the solar system. These 'pre-solar' grains are so named because they are thought to have existed before the solar system formed. They are ancient minerals that originally formed around stars such as red giants or supernovae. Stars such as these were our ancestors, providing the elements from which the solar system formed. The grains produced around these stars floated in interstellar space before being swept up and incorporated into our newly forming solar system.

RIGHT A pre-solar grain of silicon carbide, about 1 μm across, from the Murchison meteorite.

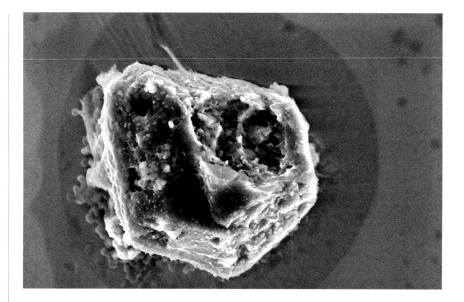

RIGHT A pre-solar grain of silicon carbide, about 1 μm across, from the Murchison meteorite.

Pre-solar grains provide unparalleled opportunities to perform astrophysics in the laboratory, to learn about element and grain-forming processes occurring in and around other stars. Studies of pre-solar grains have told us that the solar system is made up of some material from a supernova as well as material from several red giant stars. Dozens of stars separated by billions of kilometres contributed to our solar system, ultimately sitting side-by-side in a single meteoritic rock.

ORGANIC COMPOUNDS Some meteorites contain organic compounds, made up of the elements carbon, hydrogen, oxygen and nitrogen. These compounds, found most abundantly in carbonaceous chondrites, are the main constituents of

RIGHT Tranmission electron microscope (TEM) image of carbon-rich, organic globules in the Tagish Lake meteorite. The composition of the deuterium and hydrogen in these objects indicate that they have a pre-solar origin.

living things. Those found in meteorites are thought to have formed abiotically, i.e. no life was involved in their formation. Some formed in interstellar space prior to the formation of the solar system, some within the solar nebula, and perhaps some in the asteroid parent. Meteorites containing organic material probably fell to Earth before life flourished here, and may indeed have been an important first step to life beginning on Earth, by providing the basic vital ingredients needed to create living things.

HEATING OF YOUNG PLANETESIMALS

Nearly all chondrites, and certainly all melted meteorites (see p.62), show evidence of having been heated since they formed into a planetesimal. In the case of achondrites and iron meteorites, this heating event was clearly very severe, and enough to cause the rock to melt. In the case of chondrites, the extent of their alteration since formation is highly variable and this provides a secondary classification scheme for these meteorites.

Chondrites are classified by number from 1 (unheated but water damaged) to 6 (very severely heated). A few rare meteorites seem to have experienced very little heating since they formed and apparently remain almost unchanged. The most 'pristine' meteorites are usually those of Type 3. These have experienced minimal

BELOW An optical microscope image of the Parnallee (Type 3) chondrite that has experienced little heating. The chondrules are clear and well-defined. The field of view is 5 mm (¼ in).

ABOVE An optical microscope image of the Barwell (Type 6) chondrite. This meteorite has experienced a significant amount of heating, and the chondrules are not so well defined as for the Parnallee meteorite (see p.59). The field of view is 5 mm (¼ in).

heating and little alteration by water. Others (Types 1 and 2) contained a lot of water-ice when they formed. Heating on these bodies had the effect of melting the water, leaving the rocks water-damaged but not extensively heated. However, the majority of meteorites (of Types 4 and higher) have textures suggesting that they have suffered changes brought about by heat. Heating has altered the mineralogy and textures of the rocks and has caused the constituent elements to move around and become well-mixed. A tiny proportion of the heat in planetesimals is simply gravitational: as the components of the chondrites collapsed to form a larger body they released heat. However, this process cannot account for much of the heat required to produce the effects that are observed. We must look to a different mechanism, and the most likely heat source appears to be from the decay of radioactive isotopes with extremely short half-lives (i.e. unstable isotopes that decay quickly, relative to geological processes, producing energy).

Isotopic studies of meteorites show that they contained short-lived isotopes when they formed. The most important heat sources may have been the isotopes aluminium-26 and iron-60. We know that these isotopes were once active inside meteoritic material because today the meteorites contain excessive amounts of the

HOW OLD ARE METEORITES, PLANETS AND THE SOLAR SYSTEM?

Ages are measured using radioactive 'clocks'. By 'age', in the case of melted meteorites, we mean the time since the minerals cooled from a molten state to their current solid state. In the case of unmelted chondrites, this can either mean the age of the individual constituents of the meteorite or the age at which the constituents coagulated together.

Elements sometimes have more than one isotope, particles of the same element that have different masses. While many isotopes are stable and can survive intact indefinitely, some are radioactive and break down to form different isotopes and elements. The half-life, which measures the rate at which these radioactive isotopes disintegrate, is known and so by measuring the amounts of both the parent isotope and its daughter decay products present in a rock, the age of the rock can be determined. The age determined is the time from when the rock was last hot enough for its constituent isotopes to be able to move around freely. The isotopes that are most commonly used for age dating of ancient solar system rocks are rubidium-87 (which decays to strontium-87 with a half-life of 49 billion years), samarium-147 (which decays to neodynium-143) and two uranium isotopes that both decay to lead isotopes. Since most meteoritic fragments of asteroids yield similar ages (around 4.57 billion years), older than any rocks that originate on Earth, this is thought to be the age of the solar system and the planets in it.

isotopes' decay products such as magnesium-26, a decay product of aluminium-26. Many of these isotopes were present in the solar system at the levels expected for interstellar material, but some isotopes have much higher than expected abundances. A proportion of these short-lived isotopes may have formed in a stellar event, such as a supernova, that must have happened very shortly before the formation of the solar system. Others may have formed close to the young sun and were transported to the asteroid and planet-forming region in jets. However they formed, they are important because they can be used as extremely sensitive clocks of early solar system processes (see box).

Meteorites, and their components, that have a large amount of decay products, must have contained a large amount of radioactive nuclides when they originally formed. The more radioactive isotopes rocks initially contained, the older they are likely to be – in younger rocks, these isotopes would have mainly decayed away by their formation time. For example, the work of scientists Alex Halliday and D-C. Lee on the short-lived isotope hafnium-187 has been used to infer that the planet Mars formed relatively quickly – within a few tens of millions of years of the start of the solar system – because isotopic studies show that Martian rocks contained this isotope when the planet formed. In contrast, the Earth formed much later when all the hafnium-187 had already decayed away.

MELTED METEORITES

In contrast to meteorites that have experienced only limited heating or some aqueous alteration, like those previously discussed, some meteorites come from asteroids that have totally or partially melted. There are three types of melted meteorites: irons, stony-irons and achondrites. These meteorites come from planets or asteroids that have undergone differentiation. In this section we discuss those that come from asteroids.

When a chondritic asteroid is heated to its melting point (between 1,000 and 1,300°C or 1,832 and 2,372°F depending on its composition), the distribution of minerals changes dramatically. The silicate material will melt and the flecks of metal will coalesce and, because the metal is heavier than the silicate material, it will sink to the centre or core of the body even under the low gravitational forces of an asteroid. As the body gets hotter, the silicate minerals will start to melt. These first form basalt, a rock composed of plagioclase and pyroxene, and this melt will

DIFFERENTIATION PROCESS

Differentiation is the name given to a process whereby a planet or asteroid transforms from a homogeneous starting material into a core, mantle and crust based on density variations of minerals in the starting materials.

ABOVE LEFT A primitive, chondritic body before heating begins.

ABOVE RIGHT A primitive body when heating and melting has begun; the heavier minerals (in red) start to sink to the middle (core) of the body, while lighter minerals (pink) begin to float to the surface. The medium weight minerals (brown) have been heated and melted enough to allow the others to sink or float.

LEFT The body has completely separated into a core (red), mantle (brown) and crust (pink). This process, called differentiation, has taken place on all the planets in the inner solar system, including Earth's moon. It has also occurred on a number of asteroids.

ABOVE A piece of the Henbury iron meteorite, 28 cm (11 in) across, which once formed part of an asteroid's core.

rise to form the crust of an asteroid. Minerals with a medium density will form a lower layer called the mantle. This process of metal and silicate separation is called differentiation.

Based on meteorite studies, we know that some asteroids have undergone differentiation, but there are still many questions remaining about the process. For instance, how big does an asteroid need to be to melt? Was differentiation of asteroids a common process in the early solar system? If it was very common, did planets form from differentiated planetesimals, rather than primitive, unmelted ones?

The iron meteorites are composed of iron with varying amounts of nickel and are thought to represent material from the cores of differentiated asteroids. There are two types of stony-iron meteorite. The first, called pallasites, are composed of a green mineral (usually olivine) embedded in a metallic matrix. These types of meteorites are thought to be from the core–mantle boundary of differentiated asteroids. The other type of stony-iron meteorite is called a mesosiderite (which means 'half iron' in Greek). These meteorites are characterized by a jumbled mixture of basaltic and metallic material and probably formed when two molten asteroids collided. The stony melted meteorites, the achondrites, represent material from the crusts and mantles of melted asteroids. These meteorites are called achondrites to distinguish them from the other type of 'stony' meteorites, the chondrites.

IRON METEORITES

Most iron meteorites come from the cores of differentiated asteroids and are sometimes called magmatic irons. Some iron meteorites, termed non-magmatic, come from asteroids where the process of differentiation was interrupted. All iron meteorites are classified according to chemical composition and structural features. Iron meteorites are composed primarily of iron (Fe), with varying amounts of nickel (Ni), sulphur (S), carbon (C) and phosphorus (P). On the basis of the abundance of nickel and elements that occur in trace amounts (at levels of parts per million or less), around 85% of iron meteorites fit into one of 13 groups (a group contains five members or more), and probably come from 13 different parent bodies. The remaining 15% cannot be grouped so readily and may originate from up to 50 different parent bodies.

The structure of iron meteorites is seen primarily in the Widmanstätten pattern, a texture that forms during cooling from 700°C to 450°C (1,292 to 842°F), and interestingly only when the iron has become solid. When elements move between minerals while a rock is solid, it is called diffusion. To form the Widmanstätten pattern, the diffusion had to occur very slowly. This would happen if the asteroid core was well insulated and took a long time to cool. The Widmanstätten pattern is only revealed when the sample is cut and etched with a mixture of dilute nitric acid and alcohol. The pattern is named after Count Alois von Widmanstätten, who was credited with its discovery in 1808. However, the pattern was also discovered independently, some years earlier, by the chemists Edward Howard (see p.14) and William Thomson.

The iron and nickel in these meteorites forms two different minerals, one that is poor in nickel called kamacite and the other rich in nickel called taenite. Kamacite

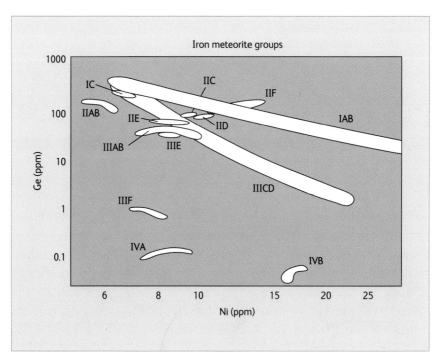

RIGHT Simplistic germanium (Ge) vs nickel (Ni) plot in different iron meteorite groups.

typically contains less than 10% nickel, while taenite can have an abundance of nickel that ranges between 25 and 50%. At high temperatures, when the metal is molten, the iron and nickel can easily mix, but when the metal becomes solid (or crystallizes) and cools these elements will form the characteristic criss-cross pattern. The thickness of the pattern gives information about the cooling history of these meteorites. A thicker pattern will form if the meteorite was cooling very slowly, which might be the case if it were in the middle of the core or under a thick silicate mantle. A thinner pattern forms if the cooling rate is more rapid.

Iron meteorites also have other minerals besides the kamacite and taenite. The most common is troilite, a sulphide of iron that is often found as rounded nodules distributed randomly throughout many iron meteorites. Minerals containing carbon and phosphorus are also quite common.

STONY-IRON METEORITES

Stony-iron meteorites are so called because they are a mixture of stony and iron material. As discussed above, there are two types of stony-iron meteorites. One group is called the pallasites. The name pallasite comes from the German scientist, Peter Simon Pallas, who described the Krasnojarsk pallasite in 1772, before it was known that this sample came from outer space. Pallasites, when sliced and polished, are perhaps the most beautiful of all the meteorites because of the mix of metal and centimetre-sized, gem-quality olivine that is called peridot. These meteorites are thought to have originated at the core–mantle boundary of large asteroids. The

ABOVE Iron meteorites, when sliced open and etched with acid, typically show a distinctive criss-cross pattern called a Widmanstätten pattern. This slice of Canyon Diablo is 15 cm (6 in) across.

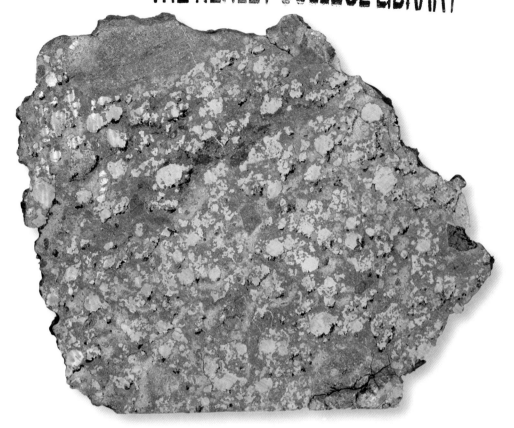

chemical composition of the metal in a few of the pallasites is similar to some iron meteorites, which suggests that they might have originated on the same type of asteroid.

The other stony-iron group is called the mesosiderites. They are composed of half iron and half silicate. In contrast to the pallasites, the silicate material found in mesosiderites is composed of igneous (or previously molten) rock and mineral fragments that formed on the crusts of differentiated asteroids. The way the metal and silicate are mixed up together gives a clue to how they formed. Because of the angular nature of the silicate fragments, the most likely formation scenario for mesosiderites is collision between two differentiated, and possibly molten, asteroids. The oxygen isotope composition of many of the rocky fragments in mesosiderites is identical to those found in the achondrite HED meteorites (see p.69), suggesting a link between these two very different meteorite types.

MELTED STONY METEORITES OR ACHONDRITES

There are three groups of stony meteorites that are not classified as chondritic, due to their lack of chondrules and metal. Their textures are igneous (compare to chondrite textures in the figures on p.47), which means they crystallized from a molten state. The three groups are not related to each other and thus represent the crusts or upper mantles of at least three different types of asteroids.

ABOVE The Estherville mesosiderite formed after a catastrophic collision between two asteroids.

OPPOSITE The Esquel pallasite, composed of gem-quality olivine crystals embedded in metal.

ANGRITES Angrites are a small group (only 17 members as of January 2009) of meteorites that are composed primarily of pyroxene and plagioclase, the mineralogy of a rock type called basalt. Basalt is a very common volcanic rock on Earth and is found in association with island volcanoes such as those in Hawaii, Iceland and the Aeolian islands off the Mediterranean coast of Italy. The angrites are an enigmatic group. The coarse textures of these meteorites indicate they may have cooled relatively slowly. But, the zoning patterns of elements in the minerals indicate relatively rapid crystallization. The debate is ongoing about what this means for the history of the parent body. A particularly interesting feature of the angrites is that they have very old ages, of around 4,556 million years, which indicates that asteroidal differentiation and igneous activity was occurring only a few million years after the solar system formed.

AUBRITES The aubrites are igneous meteorites that seem to be related to the enstatite chondrites. Unusually for meteorites, the aubrites are a light white–grey colour and have very pale, cream-coloured, fusion crusts. This is because the most abundant mineral (75–90%) is enstatite, a magnesium-rich pyroxene that is also quite abundant in the enstatite chondrites. The most likely formation scenario for aubrites is that they started out like enstatite chondrites, but their parent asteroid was heated to temperatures high enough to cause it to melt and differentiate. Aubrites contain some minerals that are exceedingly rare. An example is found in the aubrite Bustee, which contains centimetre-sized chestnut brown crystals of a mineral called oldhamite, a calcium sulphide that is not found naturally on Earth.

RIGHT The Bustee aubrite, a light-coloured meteorite containing brown oldhamite crystals.

HOWARDITE, EUCRITE, DIOGENITE (HEDS) By far the largest group of achondrites, numbering 856 as of January 2009, is the howardite, eucrite and diogenite, or HED, group. These meteorites are interesting because they are related to the asteroid 4 Vesta based on spectroscopy (as discussed on p.46).

The eucrite meteorites are basaltic in composition, composed primarily of the silicate minerals pyroxene and plagioclase. The textures of these rocks vary from quite fine-grained to relatively coarse-grained, indicating that some may have come from the surface of their parent body, while others might have been buried and allowed to cool slowly. These rocks also show evidence of mixing due to impact. Many of the meteorites in this group are breccias, rocks that are broken up and mixed together.

The diogenite meteorites are composed mostly of pyroxene, which when found on its own tells us something about how it formed. Diogenites probably formed in very thick lava flows, where the very slow cooling rate would allow the minerals within the flow to differentiate (similar to how a planet differentiates). When this happens in a lava flow, the result is that layers of minerals are built up. Pyroxene forms first in a thick lava flow and, because it is heavier than the melt, rains out to form a layer on the bottom. Diogenites probably come from this layer of accumulated pyroxene.

Finally, the howardite meteorites are breccias and contain bits of both eucrites and diogenites. These probably formed when a large impact excavated and mixed material from the surface and from deep within the parent body.

The HED meteorites, although very different from each other in mineralogy and texture, have chemical similarities that strongly suggest they formed on the same parent body. They also have links to the stony-iron mesosiderites, and, as discussed on p.67, they have strong links to the asteroid 4 Vesta.

LEFT The Sioux County eucrite, which is thought to have originated on the asteroid 4 Vesta. The sample weighs 153 g (5 ⅓ oz).

RIGHT Microscope image of the Pasamonte eucrite showing a basaltic texture. Field of view is 2.5 mm (about 1/10 in) across.

BELOW Microscope image of the Johnstown diogenite. Diogenites are coarse grained and composed primarily of one mineral, pyroxene. Field of view is 2.5 mm (about 1/10 in) across.

NOT CHONDRITE OR ACHONDRITE?

There are several groups of meteorites that fall in between chondrites and achondrites. They are very primitive chemically, but their textures indicate they have experienced heating and sometimes even extensive melting. There are four groups of meteorites that show these features. These meteorites now form a type called primitive achondrites.

LEFT Microscope image of the Lodran meteorite. This meteorite is the type specimen of the Lodranite meteorites. The lodranites are related to the acaplucoites but lodranites are more coarse-grained. Field of view is 2.5 mm (about 1/10 in) across.

ABOVE Microscope image of the Brachina meteorite, the type specimen of the Brachinite meteorites. Brachinites are composed mostly of olivine with minor amounts of pyroxene and plagioclase. Field of view is 2.5 mm (about 1/10 in) across.

BRACHINITES

Brachinites are named after the Brachina meteorite that was found in 1974 in South Australia. They are a small group of meteorites, with only 19 members as of January 2009. They contain mostly olivine, with minor amounts of pyroxene and plagioclase, as well as metal and sulphides. Their textures indicate that they experienced some heating, but it is unclear how much. The question of whether they are primitive or the product of extensive heating remains unanswered.

UREILITES

Ureilites are one of the oddest and least understood types of meteorites. They are made up of the minerals olivine and pyroxene, but also contain veins of carbon-rich materials in the form of graphite and diamond. Diamonds on Earth mostly form at extreme depths where the pressure is high enough to convert graphitic carbon to diamond. Asteroids are much smaller than the Earth, and thus do not have high enough pressures, even in the centre of the body, to create diamonds. The pressure comes from impacts in the case of meteorites. Collisions between two asteroids can create very high pressures in a short time. Such events obscure the original nature of the rocks, and unravelling the evolution pathway of these rocks is therefore difficult. Also a mystery is how these rocks formed, combining as they do, high temperature olivine and pyroxene with delicate carbonaceous material and volatile gases that must have always remained at a low temperature.

WINONAITES/IAB IRONS

The second largest group of iron meteorites, with more than 120 members, are the IAB iron meteorites. Their chemistry suggests that they do not come from a well-formed core of a differentiated asteroid. A very strange thing about these meteorites is that they contain silicate material, but unlike that in pallasites (where it is only olivine) or the mesosiderites. The silicate in these irons is very randomly distributed and is primitive (almost chondritic) in nature. The textures of the silicates show that they have been heated. The silicates found in the IAB irons are related to the stony winonaite meteorite group through oxygen isotopes, mineralogy and mineral chemistry.

The winonaites are a small group of meteorites that contain mostly low-calcium pyroxene, with smaller amounts of olivine, plagioclase, metal and sulphide. It is thought that these meteorites come from a body where the heating, melting and differentiation began, but was interrupted, most likely by a catastrophic impact. This collision mixed up bits of heated material (the metal) with unheated material to form what we see today.

BELOW A slab of the IAB iron meteorite Lueders showing the size, shapes and distribution of silicate inclusions. The slab is about 10 cm (4 in) wide.

ACAPULCOITES/LODRANITES

Named after meteorites that fell in Acapulco, Mexico, and Lodran, Pakistan, this group shows evidence for partial melting of silicate materials. The metallic portion is missing. The acapulcoites have smaller grain sizes than the lodranites. In this grouping, the acapulcoites represent the original composition, but it has been heated to lose its chondritic texture. Very thin veins of sulphide are found along silicate grain boundaries. These form at temperatures just below that which will melt silicate.

The lodranites are very coarse-grained, and some of the minerals that are found in the acapulcoites are not found in lodranites. This means these minerals melted and migrated away. The lodranites are called rock residues (the material that is left behind when some of the rock is melted and moves to another part of the asteroid).

These meteorites formed when a chondritic body was heated to a temperature that was able to melt some sulphide (c.1,000°C or 1832°F) and silicate (c.1,100°C or 2,012°F). The acapulcoites did not get as hot as the lodranites, so the temperature on the parent body was not evenly distributed.

LUNAR METEORITES

BELOW A slice of the lunar meteorite Northwest Africa 482. This meteorite is very rich in the feldspar mineral anorthite, which gives it its pale colour. Meteorites like this are believed to be derived from the Lunar highland regions. The longest edge is about 5 cm (2 in).

The moon is our nearest celestial neighbour, orbiting around the Earth nearly 400,000 km (1/4 million miles) away. It is the only astronomical body on which humans have so far set foot, and returned samples. For that reason we know more about the moon than any other body apart from the Earth. In addition to rocks returned from space missions, we also have samples of the moon that arrived on our planet by themselves, in the form of meteorites.

LEFT The Moon showing the locations of the Apollo mission landing sites.

The idea that some meteorites may have come from the moon is a very old one – more than three centuries ago some scientists suggested that *all* meteorites originated from the moon. However, the discovery of asteroids provided a new possible source. Later, results from camera networks (see p.20) showed that the vast majority of meteorites had orbits from asteroids and not from the moon. Then in 1981 an unusual meteorite was found by an American expedition in Antarctica. Allan Hills (ALH) 81005 is dark grey, containing centimetre-sized patches of white material. Once the sample was returned to the USA, it was immediately recognized as looking extremely similar to some of the Apollo samples from the moon. Since ALH 81005 was discovered, about 64 more lunar meteorites have been found. Most of these were also found in Antarctica, but one was found in Australia, and the rest in the Sahara Desert.

The dark and light material present in lunar meteorites corresponds to different minerals. Looking up to the moon on a clear night you can see that there are pale-coloured regions, called highlands (made up mostly of the calcium-rich mineral anorthite), and darker regions, called maria (made up of basalt). In lunar meteorites, the dark material consists of the minerals pyroxene, olivine and plagioclase, and the light-coloured material is mostly anorthite. The meteorites were identified as being lunar because the abundances of major and minor elements within them, matches both those measured by remote sensing of the moon and direct analyses of Apollo samples. The oxygen isotopic composition of lunar meteorites is also identical to Apollo samples. The meteorites contain abundant nitrogen and noble gases, which were implanted by the solar wind. This also suggests the meteorites came from a place such as the lunar surface that has no atmosphere to protect it from the wind blown out by the sun.

The lunar meteorites provide much extra information to supplement that from the lunar return samples. The lunar surface area sampled by all the missions to the moon only accounts for around 9% of the lunar surface. The lunar meteorites seem to come from a wider range of different regions, as they have a greater diversity in compositions, and some have originated on the far side of the moon, well away from all the previous sample sites. The areas visited by the Apollo astronauts may not be typical of the moon as a whole, and so samples from different lunar regions provide an extremely welcome addition to our knowledge of lunar geology.

RIGHT A slice of the Lunar meteorite Northwest Africa 773. This meteorite is dark in colour and composed of olivine and pyroxene and some feldspar. Meteorites like this one are believed to have originated in the basaltic, mare regions of the Moon. Length about 4.5 cm (1 ¾ in).

THE SPACE RACE

In the 1950s, the 'cold war' between the USA and USSR had become intense and the two countries were locked in competition with each other. One of the ways they wanted to assert their technical superiority was to become the first country to visit the moon – the Space Race had begun. In the early 1960s, American president J F Kennedy announced his intention to send men to the moon by the end of the decade: 'We go there not because it is easy, but because it is hard,' he said. Both countries invested heavily in their space programmes; for the Americans, this was the Apollo programme, and for the Russians, the Luna programme. In July 1969, the Americans were the first to land on the moon and returned the first samples back to Earth, the first extraterrestrial samples we had apart from meteorites. Ultimately, scientists from all over the world benefited from the political jostling between countries by gaining access to these unique samples.

THE NEW SPACE RACE

After the political impetus of the Space Race had dissipated there was little to encourage governments to return to the moon. Indeed, in the decades after Apollo, the only major lunar mission was the NASA Clementine mission, which mapped the composition of the surface of the moon. The dawn of the new millennium, however, heralded some new interest in lunar exploration, and this time many more space agencies are involved. Several countries decided to embark on voyages of discovery to our nearest neighbour. These missions include SMART-1 (European Space Agency), Kaguya or Selene (Japan), Chandrayaan-1 (India), Chang'e (China) and Lunar Reconnaissance Orbiter (USA-NASA). The aim of many of these missions is to rediscover space flight, with the objective of later exploring further out in the solar system and in some cases of trying again to take people to other planets. It is to be hoped, in our lifetimes, we will once again see people walk on other worlds.

LEFT Early morning view on 9 November 1967 of Pad A, Launch Complex 39, Kennedy Space Centre, showing Apollo 4 Saturn V prior to launch later that day. This was the first launch of the Saturn V.

THE ORIGIN AND EVOLUTION OF THE MOON

Samples from the Apollo and Luna missions, along with lunar meteorites, have allowed us to understand something of the dramatic history of the moon. The moon–Earth system is unique in the solar system because the size of the moon is so large compared to the size of the Earth. Rocks from the moon and Earth show some clear similarities but also important differences. The oxygen isotope compositions of the Earth and moon are indistinguishable, pointing to a common origin for both. However, the moon has a lot less iron than the Earth – it does not have a large iron-rich core – and it has a much lower abundance of volatile elements. In particular, it has hardly any water, in great contrast, of course, to the watery Earth.

In the 1980s, scientists brought all these facts together to produce a theory of how the moon formed, which is today widely accepted. It is called the Giant Impact Theory. In it, a planet the size of Mars, called Theia, hit the young Earth at an oblique angle. This completely melted most of both planets, and forced a ring of material to spin out of the Earth, which accreted quickly into the moon. The moon was initially extremely hot, and the outermost parts were molten, forming a 'global magma ocean', a sea of liquid rock over the whole surface of the moon. As this ocean solidified, it formed a layered structure, with the lighter anorthosite rock floating to the top. For the first few hundred million years of the moon's existence, it was subjected to extensive bombardment by asteroids, leaving many craters over its surface. Some of the giant impact basins were then filled with lava, during episodes of basaltic volcanism; these are the dark circles you can see on the surface of the moon.

BELOW The grazing impact of a Mars-size body with the proto-earth more than 4 billion years ago is believed to have led to the formation of our moon.

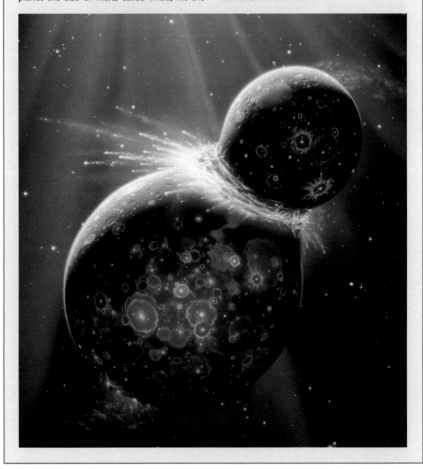

MARTIAN METEORITES

There is a group of meteorites with features that indicate they did not form on an asteroid. All the members of this group have young ages, all but one are between about 1,300 and 165 million years old. They also have igneous textures that could only crystallize from a melt. The young ages imply that these rocks come from a body that has been geologically active: one that has been hot, or even molten, for a long time. Even melted asteroids cooled off by about 4,000 million years ago because they were too small to stay hot. For rocks to be as young as 165 million years means that these came from a planet-sized body. But which planet? There are several lines of evidence that show these rocks came from Mars.

HOW DO WE KNOW THESE METEORITES ARE FROM MARS?

The Martian meteorites were known to be different from asteroidal meteorites long before they were determined to be from Mars. The lines of evidence that allowed scientists to deduce their origin are as follows.

Firstly, the textures of these rocks are all igneous. This means they formed from melted rock. There are asteroidal meteorites (see p.63) that formed from melted

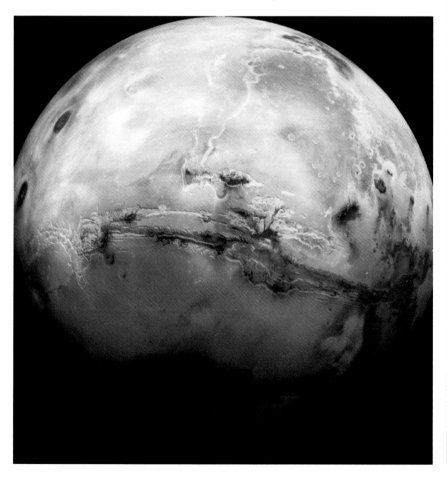

LEFT The planet Mars with the Valles Marineris trough system visible in the foreground.

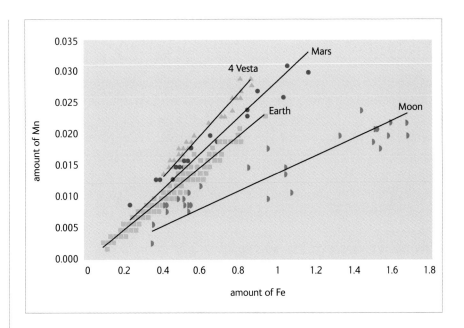

rock, so this does not definitively prove they are from Mars. Secondly, although these rocks contain the same minerals as found in asteroidal meteorites, there are differences in the ratios of some elements. The iron to manganese ratios in the olivine and pyroxene minerals, together with the oxygen isotopic composition, showed that the rocks are related to each other and came from the same parent body.

Thirdly, their ages indicate they come from a planet-sized body. The ages of all but one of these meteorites are less than 1,300 million years. The 'clocks' that record ages in meteorites start when the rock cools down from the molten state.

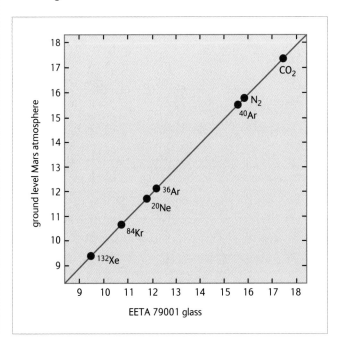

RIGHT Diagram showing that the gases trapped inside EET A79001 are the same, and in the same relative proportions, as those in Mars' atmosphere.

LEFT A cut face of meteorite EET A79001, showing the inclusions of black glass in which pockets of Mars' atmosphere are trapped. The meteorite is about 15 cm (6 in) across.

All asteroids are too small to be hot for very long, and that is why even the igneous-textured asteroidal meteorites are all 4,000 million years old or older. Young ages indicate a large body that can keep melting rocks for longer, so that means a planet. The final piece of evidence that proves these rocks are from Mars comes from the composition of gases that were trapped in the Elephant Moraine (EET) A79001 meteorite. This meteorite contains black glass in addition to the other igneous minerals. The glass formed by a shock melting, possibly during the impact that launched it from the surface of Mars. Analysis of the air trapped in the glass shows that it is identical to the composition of the air on the surface of Mars, as measured by the Viking landers in 1976. Because all the rocks are related through their mineral chemistry, ages and textures, they all must come from Mars.

Rocks are launched from Mars by the process of impact ejection. As we have discussed (chapter 3), impacts and collisions between planetary bodies are important processes. If an asteroid or comet were to hit the surface of Mars at a small enough angle and with enough speed, then ejecta from the impact could escape the gravity of Mars to orbit the sun, and some of this material can land on the Earth as meteorites. Meteorites from Mars are very rare. As of January 2009 there are 90 specimens from 42 individual meteorites. Of the Martian meteorites in the world's collections, four are falls (see chapter 1). These are Chassigny, France (1815), Shergotty, India (1865), Nakhla, Egypt (1911), and Zagami, Nigeria (1962). Interestingly, Chassigny and Zagami fell on the same day – 3 October – but 147 years apart. Most of the rest have been found in the hot deserts of Africa or Oman (62) and the cold desert of Antarctica (21). The remaining three meteorites were found in Brazil and the USA.

Martian meteorites were originally classified into one of three groups, named after three of the best-known meteorites of this type – Shergotty, Nakhla and Chassigny. Shergotty is a broadly basaltic rock composed mostly of the minerals pyroxene and plagioclase. The rocks that resemble Shergotty are called shergottites. Nakhla is classified as a clinopyroxenite, which means that it formed in the middle of a thick lava flow or a sill and represents something from a shallow depth. The rocks that resemble Nakhla are called nakhlites. Chassigny is of a very rare rock type, called a dunite, meaning it is composed almost entirely of olivine. Until very recently, no other Martian meteorites had dunitic features. Collectively the rocks were known as SNCs (after Shergotty, Nakhla and Chassigny). Then in 1994 the meteorite ALH 84001 was shown to have a Martian origin. This meteorite is very different from the other meteorites, being extremely old at 4,500 million years, and composed of orthopyroxene. This meteorite did not fit into the classic SNC scheme and therefore meteorites from Mars are now called Martian meteorites.

SHERGOTTITES

Shergottites are silicate rocks that are now divided into four subgroups. One group, the basaltic shergottites, consists of fine-grained rocks composed of equal amounts of pyroxene and plagioclase. These rocks formed in a lava flow on the surface of Mars. The other groups are more coarse-grained, which means they cooled more

RIGHT Microscope image of the Zagami shergottite. The fractures in the pyroxene mineral grains and the paler patches of glass show that the rock has been shocked. Field of view is 5 mm (¼ in).

slowly. They probably formed deeper in the Martian crust than the basaltic rocks. All of these meteorites are heavily shocked but not brecciated. The shergottites erupted onto the Martian surface between 165 and 450 million years ago. The rocks we have on Earth were launched from Mars in two different impact events between about 0.5 and 3 million years ago.

LEFT Shergottite Sayh al Uhaymir 008, found in Oman in 1999. The specimen is about 10 cm (4 in) long.

ASTEROIDAL METEORITES ON MARS

Given the cratering record on Mars, it is not unexpected that asteroidal meteorites should be on the surface of Mars too. The Mars Exploration Rovers (Spirit and Opportunity) that have been roaming around Mars since January 2004 have found such meteorites. The rovers discovered five meteorites: three at the site explored by Opportunity and two found during Spirit's traverse. Based on chemistry measurements, the meteorites are irons or mesosiderites.

LEFT Mars Exploration Rover found this iron meteorite on Mars. The pitted, basketball-size object is mostly made of iron and nickel.

NAKHLITES

Nakhlites are named after Nakhla, a meteorite that fell in Egypt in 1911. These meteorites are clinopyroxenites, meaning they are composed almost entirely of the green mineral augite. They also contain small amounts of minerals that formed in the presence of water, such as carbonates, clays and sulphates. These formed in a thick lava flow on or near the Martian surface. These meteorites are older than the shergottites, with ages of around 1,300 million years. They were also launched from the surface of Mars before the shergottites, roughly 10 to 12 million years ago.

ABOVE RIGHT The Nakhla meteorite fell as a shower of stones in Egypt in 1911. Although one of the stones is rumoured to have killed a dog, this story is almost certainly not true.

RIGHT Thin section of Nakhla meteorite (field of view is about 2.5 mm or about ¹/₁₀ in), showing large pyroxene crystals.

LEFT Thin section of Chassigny in cross-polarized light, showing shocked and deformed olivine grains. The field of view is 3 mm (1/10 in).

CHASSIGNITES

Until very recently there was only one member of the chassignite group, the meteorite Chassigny. A second meteorite has now been added to this group. These meteorites are dominated by the mineral olivine and are called dunites. This mineral is often heavy and when it forms will sink within the melted rock as it crystallizes. These rocks most likely formed at depth within the Martian surface. They have similar formation ages to the nakhlites, but it is not known if they come from the same region on Mars.

ORTHOPYROXENITE

Allan Hills (ALH) 84001 is the only member of this subgroup. It was discovered in Antarctica in 1984 and was originally classified as a diogenite (see p.68), based on its mineralogy. It was not shown to be Martian in origin until 1994. ALH 84001 is composed almost entirely of orthopyroxene, making it very different from other meteorites from Mars. It is the oldest of the Martian meteorites, at 4,500 million years. Its history is complicated by shock and thermal metamorphism. Interestingly, it contains carbonate minerals. On Earth the presence of carbonate minerals generally means a rock has come into contact with liquid water at some point in its history. The carbonates in ALH 84001, however, are complex both in their chemistry and shape, which has led to several theories about how they formed. Some think they formed at low temperature, and some think they formed at high temperature. Others say they formed during the impact event that shocked the silicate minerals. The consensus seems to be that the carbonates record a varied history of impact-driven interaction between fluid and rocks.

RIGHT A piece of the ALH 84001 orthopyroxenite. It is about 5 cm (2 in) across.

BELOW Patches of orange carbonate in ALH 84001. The field of view is about 3 mm ($^1/_{10}$ in).

ARE THERE FOSSILS IN ALH 84001?

The ALH 84001 meteorite was thrown into the limelight in 1996 when scientists from NASA's Johnson Space Centre in the USA reported finding evidence in the rock that was consistent with it containing fossils. Throughout ALH 84001 there are patches of bright orange carbonates, up to a few millimetres across. A team of scientists studied the meteorite using a variety of techniques. They found tiny structures in the carbonates that looked like fossilized bacteria.

Also associated with the carbonates were organic compounds, which could have confirmed that the tiny structures were biological in origin. However, these organic compounds have been proved to be contamination from the Earth. In spite of that, the report of possible fossils in a meteorite has triggered a whole new area of research called astrobiology, dedicated to understanding the interactions between biology and planetary geology.

The investigations of ALH 84001 and the development of astrobiology have revitalized the Mars Exploration Program, which, among other things, is attempting to answer the question of whether there are habitable environments on Mars. This led to the launch of the Mars Exploration Rovers (MERs) and other missions (there are currently four missions in orbit or on the ground at Mars, with several more in the planning stages). While out traversing the surface of Mars, one of the rovers found a rock that was named Bounce Rock. This rock is chemically similar to EET A79001, the rock from which the gas that matched the atmosphere of Mars was extracted, and thus indirectly ALH 84001 helped prove that this group of meteorites on Earth was from Mars.

BELOW Scanning electron microscope image (size about 1 μm) of the surface of the orange carbonates in ALH 84001, showing what was termed a 'microfossil'.

COMETS

THE VAST MAJORITY OF METEORITES come from asteroids (>99.4%), a few come from the moon (0.4%) and a few from the planet Mars (0.2%). A very rare type of unmelted meteorite, the CI chondrites – of which only nine are known (< 0.03% of known meteorites) – have characteristics that suggest they may have originated from comets.

Comets are very important constituents of the solar system and provide scientists with evidence of the chemical and environmental conditions that existed during the very earliest stages of solar system formation. They must have formed beyond the nebula 'frost' or 'snow line', where the temperature was low enough for water-ice to form. Comets are the preserved remnants from these very cold, ice-bearing regions that composed 99% of the solar nebula disc from which our solar system formed. They are mixtures of both nebular and pre-solar materials that accreted over a vast area of the very young solar system, and thus they record the different chemical, temperature and physical environments over a vast area of space.

OPPOSITE Comet Hale-Bopp which appeared in the night skies of the northern hemisphere in 1997.

BELOW An impression of the Leonid meteor shower of November 1799, so-called because the meteors appear to radiate from the constellation Leo.

METEOR SHOWERS

As we learnt in chapter 1, approximately 40,000–60,000 t of extraterrestrial material lands on Earth every year, the majority of which is in the form of tiny dust grains usually less than 1 mm ($^1/_{25}$ in) in size; importantly, most of this dust is believed to originate from comets.

Every time a comet approaches the sun it loses material; the ices melt and vaporize, releasing trapped dust and larger particles. Typically a comet loses up to 0.1% of its mass each time it passes close to the sun. Calculations showed that Comet Halley lost about 500 million tonnes during its last orbit around the sun. Based on this amount

ABOVE A time lapse photograph taken during the Leonid meteor shower in 2001.

of mass loss, Comet Halley will only survive for another 2,200 orbits, or another 167,000 years or so. In fact, it is unlikely that Comet Halley will even last for this relatively short amount of time; most comets break up rather than shed mass linearly, so it is likely to fragment long before it 'runs out of steam'.

Direct evidence from spacecraft such as Giotto and Stardust, as well as observations of meteors, indicate that particles of 1 mm (1/25 in) and larger can make up a large proportion of the material ejected from the comet. Sometimes very large particles and fragments, a metre or larger, may also be ejected. Over time, gravity and solar radiation smear out this material so that eventually it occupies the whole of the comet's orbit around the sun. In some cases, the Earth's orbit will coincide with a cometary orbit. When the Earth encounters this cometary debris it produces a meteor shower as the larger particles burn up in the atmosphere; no material hits the ground as a meteorite. However, very tiny dust grains, usually less than 1 mm (1/25 in) in size, can reach Earth's surface; it is important to remember that these do not produce meteors as they are too small, and they simply 'float' down through the atmosphere. Interestingly, some particles from the Comet Grigg-Skjellerup have been collected by NASAs scientific aircraft flying at very high altitudes.

RIGHT A transmission electron microscope image (TEM) of a cometary particle from the Grigg-Skjellerup comet. This particle was collected by a high-altitude NASA aircraft.

50 nm

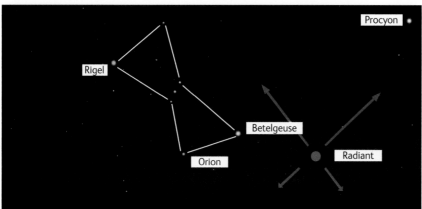

ABOVE AND LEFT Illustrations showing the radiants of the Geminid and Orionid meteors, so named as they appear to originate near to these constellations.

Every year there are several meteor showers, some of which can produce impressive meteors easily visible to the naked eye. Meteor showers are named after the stellar constellation from which, or near to which, they appear to originate. For example, the Orionids appear to radiate from the constellation of Orion and the Geminids from the constellation of Gemini.

COMET SHOWERS IN 2010

Shower name	Date	Maximum	Approx. no. meteors per hour at maximum	Parent comet
Quadrantids	1 – 5th Jan	3rd – 4th Jan	100	2003 EH1
Lyrids	16 – 25th April	21st – 22nd Apr	10	C/Thatcher
Eta Aquarids	19th April – 28th May	5 – 6th May	40-85	1P/Halley
Capricornids	3rd Jul – 15th Aug	29th – 30th Jul	15	?
Southern Delta Aquarids	18th Jul – 18th Aug	28th – 29th Jul	20	?
Perseids	23rd Jul – 20th Aug	12th – 13th Aug	60	109P/Swift-Tuttle
Draconids	6th – 10th Oct	8th – 9th Oct	10	21P/Giocobini-Zinner
Orionids	7th Oct – 7th Nov	20th – 24th Oct	25	1P/Halley
Leonids	10th – 21st Nov	17th – 18th Nov	20-40	55P/Tempel-Tuttle
Geminids	7th – 17th Dec	14th Dec	120	3200 Phaethon

Some of the major meteor showers visible to the naked eye in 2010 are shown in the table above, and the dates for future years should be very similar. While the date range for the meteor showers is predictable, the date of maximum intensity and the number of meteors seen is variable. Similarly, some showers are visible from only some parts of the world. Local astronomical societies will be able to provide more detailed information if you are interested in finding out the dates for any showers visible in your location.

As mentioned above, although the dates of the showers are predictable, the intensity (number of meteors seen, brightness etc.) can be highly variable. This is because the intensity depends on where the comet is in its journey around the sun and whether the stream has just been 'recharged' with debris from a recent passage. For example, the Leonid shower, which occurs in mid-November, is related to the Comet 55P/Tempel-Tuttle, which has a 33-year orbital period.

Historical records show that there were spectacular storms in 1833 (where hundreds of thousands of meteors per hour were reported) and in 1866 and 1867. However, the shower of 1899 was a disappointment and another spectacular storm was not observed until 1966. Astronomers predicted that the shower of 1999 would be similarly stunning, and over 3,000 meteors per hour were recorded in some locations.

LEFT Comet McNaught, a particularly bright and spectacular comet which was discovered in August 2006. This comet was only visible during January and February 2007 to observers in the southern hemisphere.

COMETS THROUGHOUT HISTORY

BELOW Chinese astronomers recorded detailed observations of comets and other celestial phenomena.

Throughout history comets have fascinated and often frightened peoples around the world. The appearance of a comet was frequently seen as a 'message from the gods' or a portent, predicting (usually negatively) major events such as wars, disease or the death of a leader. After the appearance of a comet in about AD 60, the Roman populace assumed that this meant bad news for eminent people, especially the most eminent, the Emperor Nero. On the advice of an astrologer, Nero decided to massacre a large number of the Roman nobility as this was a good way to 'deflect' the wrath of the gods! Of course, one may presume that it could also be a 'good way' to get rid of any potential rivals to the throne! Nero survived and the Roman citizens' cometary-induced superstitions were confirmed by the deaths of many important people.

Chinese astronomers also took the observation and recording of comets very seriously. Observations of astronomical phenomena were of great interest to the Emperors of China, who viewed the appearance of comets, eclipses and other phenomena with great superstition. The detailed records of Chinese astronomers include the observations in AD 1054 of a 'new star', which was actually a stellar explosion or supernova (the remnants of which can still be seen today as the Crab Nebula), and also the appearance of Comet Halley in AD 837. Comet Halley also appears in two famous European artistic works, the Bayeux Tapestry and Giotto's painting 'Adoration of the Magi', both of which depict important historical events – the Norman conquest of England in 1066 and the birth of Jesus Christ.

RIGHT The appearance of Comet Halley in 1066 was seen as an omen and recorded in the Bayeux Tapestry (see top right-hand corner).

The painting 'Adoration of the Magi' depicts Comet Halley as the 'Star of Bethlehem'. In 1985 the European Space Agency sent a mission to study Comet Halley, which was named 'Giotto' after the painter of this picture, Giotto di Bondone (1267-1337).

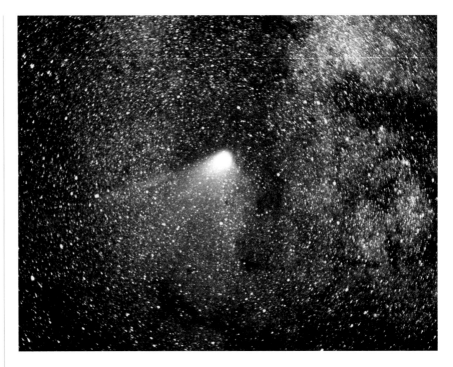

The word comet is derived from the Greek word 'kome', which means 'hair of the head'. Aristotle, the famous Greek natural philosopher first described comets as 'aster kometes', meaning 'stars with (long) hair', which was later shortened to 'kometes'. It is not surprising that Aristotle chose this word to describe his observations as the most notable feature of a comet is the long tail that streams away from the bright head or nucleus.

WHERE DO COMETS COME FROM?

Comets are classified into two types on the basis of the length of time it takes to complete an orbit of the sun, known as the comet's period. Long-period (LP) comets take more than 200 years to orbit the sun and short-period (SP) less than 200 years. Short-period comets can be further subdivided into Halley-type comets (periods of 30 to 200 years) and Jupiter-family comets (periods of less than 30 years).

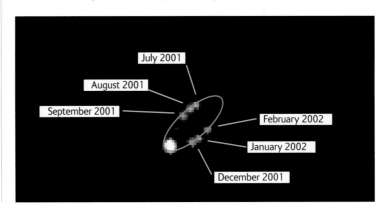

IS PLUTO A PLANET?

In 2006, the 2,500 astronomers at the annual meeting of the International Astronomical Union voted to reclassify Pluto as a 'dwarf planet'. Pluto was discovered in 1930 by the American astronomer Clyde Tombaugh and, prior to 2006, was considered to be the ninth and outermost planet of the solar system. However, its classification as a planet has been a matter of debate since Tombaugh's discovery. Pluto has some rather unusual characteristics for a 'traditional' planet. Its orbit is highly tilted compared with the other planets. Also, its orbit is highly eccentric, at times it is closer to the sun than its neighbour Neptune, and finally it is considerably smaller than the other planets, especially in comparison to the outer planets with which it is most associated. Indeed, our own moon and some of the moons of Jupiter and Saturn are larger than Pluto. Pluto's relegation to dwarf planet status was on the cards since the early 1990s, with the first observations of large Kuiper Belt or Trans-Neptunian Objects.

BELOW Illustration showing the relative sizes of the Earth, moon and TNOs and KBOs, including Pluto, which is no longer designated as a planet.

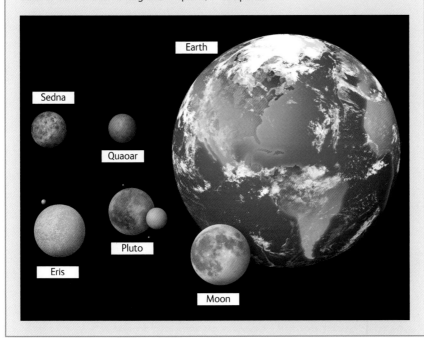

Jupiter-family comets are so named because the furthest part of their orbit from the sun (the aphelion) reaches to the orbit of Jupiter.

Comets are unstable near the sun, and where their orbits can be disrupted by the gravitational action of planets. There are two major reservoirs where comets can survive and are 'stored' without the detrimental effects of solar heating or gravitational perturbations. Long-period comets have elliptical orbits and approach the sun from random directions. The main reservoir for long-period comets is the Oort Cloud, which is believed to exist at the outermost edge of the solar system, well beyond the orbit of Pluto. As it is so very far away, comets in the Oort Cloud cannot be observed by telescopes. However, theoretical calculations by the Dutch astronomer Jan Hendrik Oort suggested that it may be the source region for long-period comets.

Short-period comets approach the sun at fairly shallow angles and were once thought to be long-period comets that had been perturbed by the gravitational fields of the giant planets into short-period orbits. It is now known that short-period comets actually originate in their own reservoir, the Kuiper Belt (or Edgeworth–Kuiper Belt). As with the Oort Cloud, the existence of the Kuiper Belt was first proposed on the basis of theoretical calculations of short-period comet orbits. The Kuiper Belt exists in a region beyond the orbit of Neptune, at a distance of between 30 and 50 AU (1 AU, or astronomical unit, is the average distance from the Earth to the sun, or about 150 million kilometres). With technical advances in telescope design and capabilities the first Kuiper Belt object was discovered by astronomers in 1992; it was an object with a diameter of about 320 km (199 miles) at a distance of 44 AU. By the end of 2008 nearly 1,100 Kuiper Belt objects had been observed, and it is estimated that tens of thousands exist in this region.

It should be noted that there is some controversy over the naming of the Kuiper Belt. Its existence was first suggested in 1930 by Frederick C. Leonard, an American astronomer who, coincidentally, also had a great interest in meteorites, and was a founding member of the Meteoritical Society. In 1949, the British astronomer Kenneth Edgeworth discussed the possibility that in the region beyond Neptune, very early solar system materials would condense into many small bodies rather than planet-sized bodies. A couple of years later, in 1951, the Dutch astronomer Gerard Kuiper proposed that bodies no longer existed in this region as they would have been thrown out of the solar system by the influence of Pluto's gravity (at the time Pluto was thought to be the same size as the Earth). Over the following years many other astronomers joined the debate with variations of the hypothesis describing a belt of material existing beyond Neptune's orbit. Today, many astronomers use the term Trans-Neptunian Object to describe the objects existing in the very outer regions of the solar system.

COMETARY NUCLEI

In the 1950s, the British astronomer Fred Whipple coined the term 'dirty snowball' to describe a comet's nucleus, and as an approximation this is still a good description. From observations by spacecraft and powerful telescopes we know that the nucleus of a comet is composed primarily of ices with rock, dust and also organic materials. Water-ice is the major component of a comet's nucleus, but other frozen compounds are also present, including carbon dioxide, methane, carbon monoxide and ammonia. The rock and dust portion is composed of silicates such as olivine and pyroxene, many of which lack a crystalline structure so are termed amorphous. Up to around 20% of the nucleus may be made up of organic compounds like ethanol, formaldehyde and methanol. The dust grains are coated with the organic compounds and mixed with the water and other volatile compound ices to form a highly porous body with voids and cracks from which jets of gas can escape.

In 1985, the European Space Agency's Giotto mission visited Comet Halley and captured, for the first time, high-resolution images of a comet's nucleus. These

An image of Comet Halley's nucleus taken by the Giotto spacecraft.

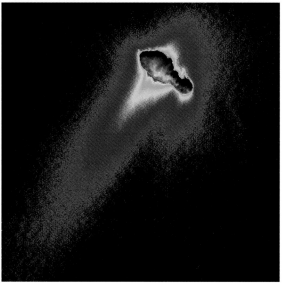

A false-colour composite image of Comet Borrelly's nucleus taken by the NASA Deep Space 1 spacecraft. The image shows jets escaping from the nucleus and the coma surrounding it.

STUDYING COMETS – SPACE MISSIONS AND TELESCOPES

The properties of comets have been measured using ground-based telescopes and dedicated spacecraft, and by analyzing cometary dust particles collected by high-altitude aircraft. Beginning in the early 1970s, telescopes analyzing the infrared spectra of comets have shown the presence of tiny grains of silicate minerals. Mass spectrometers on the Giotto mission to Comet Halley showed that, on the basis of chemical composition, there were three main types of dust present – carbon, hydrogen, oxygen and nitrogen (CHON) dominated; silicate dominated (silicon, magnesium, iron and oxygen); and mixed grains with CHON and silicate compositions. In 1999, NASA launched the Stardust mission to intercept Comet Wild/2 in January 2004. The spacecraft travelled over 4 billion km (2,500 billion miles) to collect cometary dust particles in its aerogel collector and return them

safely to Earth in January 2006. Analyzes of the collected particles by hundreds of scientists from around the world have revealed some exciting and unexpected results. Much of the silicate dust that was collected was crystalline; this was surprising as astronomical observations suggested that the silicates should be mainly glassy or amorphous. Perhaps one of the most remarkable results was the presence of a grain that was very similar in composition to a calcium and aluminium-rich inclusion or CAI (see chapter 4). CAIs were formed in very high temperatures, in the inner parts of the solar system, so it was very surprising to find one in a comet, which formed in the cold, outer regions of the solar system. This one result has shown that the young solar system was a very dynamic place, with large-scale mixing of material from the inner to the outer solar system.

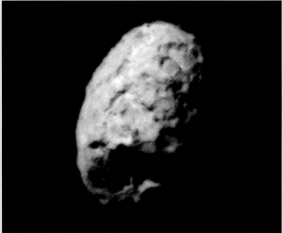

LEFT Engineers investigating the Stardust spacecraft prior to its launch in 1999. The white conical-shaped object at the top is the sample return capsule that returned the cometary particles to Earth in January 2006.
ABOVE An image of the nucleus of the Wild 2 comet, taken during a close approach by the Stardust spacecraft. The nucleus is about 5 km (3 miles) in diameter.
BELOW A cometary particle track collected in aerogel. The particle collected from this track has been named 'Inti' and has a similar composition to CAIs.

In 2005, NASA launched a further cometary mission, Deep Impact, to Comet Tempel 1. This mission was designed both to take images of the comet's nucleus and also to launch a projectile into the surface. The aim was to make a crater that could be mapped and imaged by the spacecraft to determine the interior composition of the nucleus. The projectile successfully impacted the nucleus, but the large amount of dust that was produced during the impact obscured the view of the impact crater (though the Stardust spacecraft is now being used to revisit Tempel 1 to view the crater). Results showed that the nucleus was dustier than expected and also that it was extremely porous, with about 75% empty space.

In 2004, the European Space Agency launched the Rosetta mission, which will take 10 years to travel 790 million km (491 million miles) to intercept with Comet Churyumov-Gerasimenko. The mission is, to date, the most complex ever designed to study the make-up of a comet. The orbiter will take high-resolution images, and instruments will measure the composition of the coma, tail and nucleus. The orbiter will also release a lander on to the nucleus, which will take images and analyze the composition of the ice, gas and dust on the surface.

ABOVE Images taken by the Deep Impact spacecraft at the time of projectile impact on and 16 seconds afterwards (right). A plume of ejected material can be seen in the later image.
BELOW Artist's impression of the Rosetta lander 'Philae' on the nucleus of Comet 67P/Churyumov-Gerasimenko. Owing to the nucleus' weak gravity the lander uses a 'harpoon' to prevent it escaping from the surface.

images showed the nucleus had a very irregular shape. Irregular shapes are extremely common and probably result from a combination of factors, including the low mass (and therefore gravity) of the nucleus, the loss of volatile gases and fragmentation of the nucleus during previous orbits. Further observations have shown that comet nuclei can range in size from a few hundred metres to over 40 km (25 miles) in diameter.

With an object that is composed primarily of ice you may expect the surface of the nucleus to be very bright and shiny. However, observations show that the surface is in fact very dark, and comet nuclei are some of the darkest objects that are observed in our solar system. Cometary nuclei reflect less than 4% of the sunlight that falls on them; in comparison a full moon reflects about 15%. The nuclei may be coated with a dark, tar-like substance, formed through the cosmic irradiation of the organic compounds.

COMETARY TAILS

As already mentioned, perhaps the most characteristic and spectacular feature of a comet is its tail. In fact, a comet actually has two tails, one made from dust and the other – the ion or plasma tail – from charged particles. Both tails point away from the sun, as the dust and charged particles are pushed away by solar radiation pressure.

As a comet approaches the sun the dark-crusted nucleus is heated, and the ices

BELOW Diagram of a comet showing the nucleus, coma, plasma or ion tail and the dust tail.

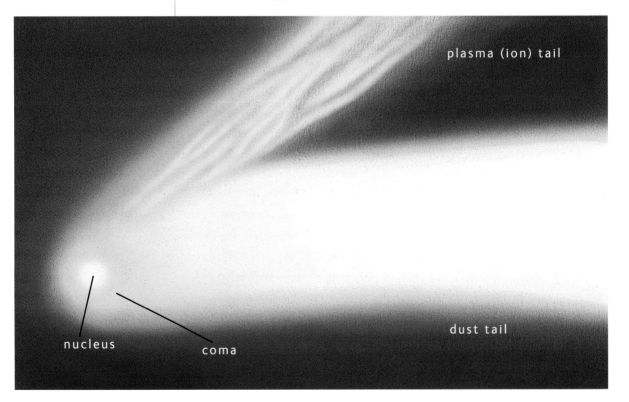

plasma (ion) tail

dust tail

nucleus

coma

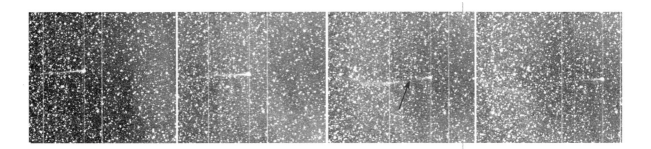

start to vaporize and release gas, dust and rock fragments into space. This escaping material forms a weak atmosphere around the nucleus termed the coma, which can be up to 10 million km (6,250 million miles) in size. A coma will appear when the comet is between 3 and 5 AU from the sun.

The gases released from the comet become ionized by the effect of solar ultraviolet radiation and are swept away by the solar wind at speeds of between 300 and 500 km/s (c. 670,000 and 1,200,000 mph), forming the ion tail. The ion tail is usually bluish in colour and is long and straight, stretching over 100 million km (62,100 million miles) in space. Magnetic fields within the ion tail, and their interaction with the solar wind, result in complex structures being formed, which are often observed as lines or ridges in the tail. In some cases the interactions of the magnetic fields can become so intense that the ion tail is 'ripped off' the comet. This happened with Comet Encke in April 2007.

In contrast to the ion tail, the dust tail looks off-white, pinkish or yellowish in colour, caused by sunlight reflecting off the dust grains. The dust tail appears curved, as a result of the individual dust grains being in the same orbit around the sun as the comet. Like the ion tail, the dust tail can reach over 100 million km (62,100 miles) in length. The grains that make up the dust tail are usually very small, less than 1 μm in size, and are coated with organic compounds. These dust particles are pushed into space, at speeds of several kilometres per second, by the expanding gases that are released from the comet as the nucleus heats up.

ABOVE In April 2007, when Comet Encke was travelling within the orbit of Mercury, a coronal mass ejection from the sun ripped its tail off. This spectacular event was captured by the NASA STEREO satellite.

SUMMARY

I N THE 200 YEARS OR SO SINCE METEORITES became the objects of serious scientific investigation, scientists have gathered a wealth of information to help us better understand how our solar system and the bodies within it, formed and evolved to their present state. We recognize that meteorites that fall to Earth come from the asteroid belt, the moon, Mars and perhaps even comets. We've learned that impacts and collisions between comets, asteroids and planets within the solar system have played a crucial part in the geological and, in the case of Earth, the biological evolution of those bodies.

Through the study of the unmelted, chondritic meteorites we can date the 'birth' of the solar system to 4,568 million years ago, and calculate the formation ages of the very first materials to condense and solidify from the hot gases and dust in the earliest stages of solar system's history. Some chondritic meteorites contain materials formed before our solar system was even born, and provide information on the birth and death of stars that existed before our sun. Melted meteorites, the iron, stony-iron and achondrite meteorites, provide us with information and clues as to how the first stages of planet formation occurred, and also how bodies such as our moon and the planet Mars formed and evolved over their history. Lunar meteorites allow scientists to study the diversity of the moon's geology; we have meteorites from areas of the moon, which were not visited by the Apollo astronauts or the unmanned Luna missions. Although many successful robotic missions have been sent to Mars and returned data on the geology of the planet, no missions have returned actual samples from Mars. Martian meteorites are the only samples of this fascinating world we have to study in laboratories on Earth, and they have provided information that is complementary to current space missions and have played an important part in the planning and development of future missions.

All of these factors and numerous others have allowed scientists to gather evidence to better understand our solar system, through its birth and development over nearly 5 billion years of history. If we have a better understanding of our own solar system, we can apply this knowledge to other star and planetary systems within our own galaxy and perhaps beyond. So, in the next few years of meteorite research, what questions remain unanswered or need clarification? What further secrets are

OPPOSITE An artist's impression of the European Space Agency ExoMars Rover, which is anticipated to land on Mars in 2016. Rovers such as these are designed to act as robotic 'geologists' and 'biologists' carrying out surveys of the planet Mars to better understand its geological history and the possibility of life existing on the red planet.

ABOVE Artist's impression of the how planet Gliese 581 c may look. This extrasolar planet or 'exoplanet' orbits the red dwarf star Gliese 581, 20.3 light years from Earth. Increased understanding of our own solar system, its formation and subsequent history will allow us to better understand planetary systems around other stars.

RIGHT Artist's impression of a hydroponic growth lab on Mars. For long-term human exploration of Mars, astronauts will have to use laboratories like this one to grow fresh fruit and vegetables to ensure a balanced and nutritious diet, helping them to cope with the rigours of living and working on Mars.

waiting to be revealed through the dedicated work of researchers around the world? Increases in analytical capabilities should open up a new world to us. Scientists will be able to investigate ever smaller samples, such as tiny interstellar grains, perhaps composed of just a few tens of atoms of carbon, nitrogen and silicon. The study of this type of material will allow better understanding of the different astrophysical processes that may have occurred, even before the birth of our own solar system. More precise instrumentation will result in the refinement of the chronology of early solar system processes, allowing us to develop more robust timescales to date processes such as accretion and parent-body processes such as aqueous alteration, metamorphism and differentiation.

With many more meteorites waiting to be found in the hot and cold deserts, it is more than likely that we will uncover distinct new meteorite types, broadening the diversity of extraterrestrial material currently known. The current classification of meteorites suggests that there are 'gaps' within and between different meteorite families and groups, so it is possible that the 'missing' link meteorites may one day be discovered.

In parallel with astronomical observations of other planetary systems, we should be able to address the questions of whether our solar system is unusual. In particular, why has the solar system been successful in creating a planet that supports life, and is it likely we will find similar life elsewhere?

Robotic missions are in the planning stages to visit asteroids and Mars, to pick up samples of these bodies and return them safely to Earth. These missions will provide a 'ground truth', and allow direct comparisons between remote-sensing observations of these bodies and the wealth of information we have gathered from the study of meteorites derived from these bodies. Both NASA and ESA highlight these 'sample return missions' as being important strategic missions as part of our further exploration of the solar system, with the hope of sending astronauts to Mars in the future. This feeds back into allowing us to reinterpret what we thought we knew about meteorites in a new light, and will pose a next generation of questions.

If we have learnt one thing from our study of meteorites it is that for every question or problem that is answered, there are still many, many more to work on. Meteoritics is an evolving science. In many ways, it is still young and in other ways more mature. We've learned a great deal from the study of meteorites over the past 200 years and that knowledge has now driven the evolution of meteoritics from a primarily lab-based, geology-chemistry discipline into one that is part of an exciting future of planetary science, with the ability to visit many of these objects that we've only been able to study indirectly for so many years.

FURTHER INFORMATION

BOOKS

A Color Atlas of Meteorites in Thin Section, D. S. Lauretta and M. Killgore. Golden Retriever Publications, Tucson and Southwest Meteorite Press, Payson, 2005. ISBN: 0-9720472-1-2.

David Levy's Guide to Observing and Discovering Comets, David Levy. Cambridge University Press, 2003. ISBN: 978-052152051.

David Levy's Guide to Observing Meteors, David Levy. Cambridge University Press, 2007.
ISBN: 978-0521696913.

Field Guide to Meteors and Meteorites, O. R. Norton. Springer, 2008. ISBN: 978-1848001565.

Mars 3-D: A Rover's-eye View of the Red Planet, Jim Bell. Sterling, 2008. ISBN: 978-1402756207.

Meteorites: A Journey Through Space and Time, Alex Bevan and John R. deLaeter. Smithsonian, 2002. ISBN: 978-1588340214.

Meteorites and Their Parent Planets, Harry Y. McSween Jr. Cambridge University Press, 2nd edn., 1999. ISBN: 978-0521587518.

Meteorites: A Petrologic, Chemical and Isotopic Synthesis, Robert Hutchison. Cambridge University Press, 2007. ISBN: 978-0521035392.

Meteorites: Their Impact on Science and History, Brigitte Zanda and Monica Rotaru. Cambridge University Press, 2001. ISBN: 978-0521799409.

Rocks from Space: Meteorites and Meteorite Hunters, O. Richard Norton. Mountain Press Publishing Company, 1998. ISBN: 978-0878423736.

Roving Mars: Spirit, Opportunity, and the Exploration of the Red Planet, Steve Squyres. Hyperion, 2006. ISBN: 978-1401308513.

Search for Life, Monica Grady. Natural History Museum, London, 2001. ISBN: 978-0565091576.

The Moon, Michael Carlowicz. Harry N. Abrams, Inc., 2007. ISBN: 978-0810993075.

WEBSITES
Information on meteorites:
American Museum of Natural History – http://www.amnh.org/exhibitions/permanent/meteorites/
Arizona State University, USA – http://meteorites.asu.edu/
Australian Museum Online – http://www.austmus.gov.au/geoscience/meteors/meteorites.htm
Museum of Victoria, Australia – http://museumvictoria.com.au/discoverycentre/infosheets/meteorites/
NASA – http://ares.jsc.nasa.gov/
National Natural History Museum, Paris (in French) – http://www.mnhn.fr/expo/meteorite/
Natural History Museum, London – http://www.nhm.ac.uk/nature-online/space/meteorites-dust/

Comets and meteors:
American Meteor Society – http://www.amsmeteors.org/
International Meteor Agency – http://www.imo.net/
Society for Popular Astronomy, UK – http://www.popastro.com/sections/comet.htm
    http://www.popastro.com/sections/meteor.htm

The solar system and space missions:
European Space Agency – http://www.esa.int/esaMI/Aurora/
    http://www.esa.int/SPECIALS/Rosetta/index.html
NASA – http://marsprogram.jpl.nasa.gov/   http://solarsystem.nasa.gov/deepimpact/index.cfm
    http://stardust.jpl.nasa.gov/home/index.html   http://www.nasa.gov/topics/moonmars/index.html

Note that website addresses are subject to change.

INDEX

PICTURE CREDITS

Front and back covers: © NHMPL; p.2 © Dr Fred Espenak/Science Photo Library

WHAT ARE METEORITES?

p6 © Pichugin Dmitry; p.7 © The Natural History Museum; p.8 top left © NASA/JSC; top right © Matt Genge; bottom © British Antarctic Survey/ Science Photo Library; p.9 top © NASA; bottom © NHMPL; p.10 © NHMPL; p.11 © Dr. Svend Buhl / www.meteorite-recon.com; p.12 bottom © Philippe Thomas; pp.13–14 © NHMPL.

WHERE ARE METEORITES FOUND?

p.16 © Gretchen Benedix; pp.17–19 © The Natural History Museum; p.20 © Phil Bland; p.21 bottom left © J.C. Bridges, J. P. Schwanethal, M. Paton, V.K. Pearson, R.C. Greenwood, J.S. Watson and G.H. Morgan, A Very Public Fireball. *Astronomy and Geophysics*, 2004, 45, 6.25–6.26; bottom right © The Natural History Museum. Redrawn from the original in Spurn, P, Oberst, J and Heinlein, D, Photographic observations of Neuschwanstein, a second meteorite from the orbit of the Pr caronibram chondrite. *Nature*, 2003, 423, 151–153; p.24 bottom Mike Eaton © The Natural History Museum; pp.24–25 © 2003/2004 ANSMET Reconnaissance Team; p.25 top © Tony Meunier; bottom © USGC; p.26 © NHMPL; p.27 © The Natural History Museum.

IMPACTS AND COLLISIONS

p.28 © David Parker/Science Photo Library; p.29 bottom left © NASA; bottom middle, right © ESA; p.30 © The Natural History Museum; p.31 © NASA/ NSSDC/Goddard Space Flight Center; p.32 Lisa Wilson © The Natural History Museum. Redrawn from the original in Simon et al., The fall, recovery, and classification of the Park Forest meteorite. *Meteoritics & Planetary Science*, The Meteoritical Society, 2004, 39, 625–634; p.33 © Ria Novosti/Science Photo Library; p.34 © George Burnside. Courtesy of the Lunar and Planetary Institute; p.35 top © Dr Rob Hough, Western Australian Museum; bottom © Luigi Folco; p.36 © Kerry Klein; p.37 issued by the Soviet Union, 20 November 1957; p.38 top © Hans Betlem, Dutch Meteor Society; bottom © Walt Radomsky; p.39 © The Natural History Museum. Redrawn from the original by ESA. p.40 © The Natural History Museum. Redrawn from the original. Image © NASA/JPL-Caltech, modified by David Fuchs. p.41 © The Natural History Museum. Redrawn from the original by Professor Richard P. Binzel, MIT.

SOURCES AND TYPES OF METEORITES

p.42 © NHMPL; p.34 © NASA, Jet Propulsion Laboratory and ESA, image by C.Carreau; p.44 top © JAXA; p.47 NHMPL; p.48 © Cambridge University Press; p.49 Mike Eaton © The Natural History Museum; p.50 © NASA-JPL; p.51 © ESO; pp.52–53 © NHMPL; p.54 © NASA Goddard Space Flight Center (NASA-GSFC); pp.55-56 © NHMPL; p.57 © Martin Lee; p.58 top © Rhonda Stroud, US Naval Research Laboratory; bottom © Keiko Nakamura. Originally reproduced in Zolensky, M E, Tomita, S, Nakashima, S, Tomeoka, K. Hollow organic globules in the Tagish Lake meteorite as possible products of primitive organic reactions, *Intl. Journal of Astrobiology*, 2002,1, 179–189; pp.59–60 © NHMPL; p.62 © The Natural History Museum. Redrawn from the original by Cascadia Meteorite Lab and Frank D. Granshaw, Artemis Science; p.63 NHMPL; p.64 Redrawn from the original in Schröder, C, et al.Meteorites on Mars observed with the Mars Exploration Rovers, *J. Geophys. Res.*, 113; pp.65–74 © NHMPL; p.75 © Luc Viatour; p.76 © NHMPL; p.77 © NASA; p.78 © Joe Tucciarone; p.79 © NASA/NSSDC/Goddard Space Flight Center; p.80 © The Natural History Museum; p.81 © NASA/JSC; p.82 © NHMPL; p.83 top © NHMPL; bottom © NASA/JPL/Cornell ; pp.84–85 © NHMPL; p.86 © NASA/JPL/Caltech.

COMETS

p.88 © Jerry Lodriguss/Science Photo Library; p.89 From 'The Midnight Sky', Edward Dunkin, 1872; p.90 top © Dr Fred Espenak/Science Photo Library; bottom © NASA/JSC; p.91 created using www.stellarium.org; p.92 © Sebastian Deiries (ESO); p.94 top © NASA; bottom © Mary Evans Picture Library; p.95 © 1990 Photo Scala, Florence; p.96 top © NASA; bottom © NASA and C. Veillet (CFHT); p.99 top © ESA; bottom © NASA-JPL; p.100 top left © NASA-KSC; top right © NASA-JPL; bottom © NASA/JPL-Caltech; p.101 top left, right © NASA/JPL-Caltech/UMD; bottom © ESA, image by AOES Medialab; p.102 © The Natural History Museum; p.103© NASA.

SUMMARY

p.104 © ESA - AOES Medialab; p.106 top © ESO; bottom © ESA – AOES Medialab.

NHMPL, Natural History Museum Picture Library

Every effort has been made to contact and accurately credit all copyright holders. If we have been unsuccessful, we apologise and welcome correction for future editions and reprints.

ACKNOWLEDGEMENTS

With thanks to Tim McCoy (National Museum of Natural History, Smithsonian, USA) for providing very useful comments and suggestions on early versions of the text. Thanks also to Kirsten Pansegrouw and Camilla Wilkinson for their helpful comments and reading of the manuscript and also to Malcolm Penn for assistance with GIS and maps.